Strong Tea & Biscuits

Strong Tea & Biscuits

True tales to encourage and inspire

VERA WATERS

Penn Cottage Books

ISBN 9780951695241

A CIP record for this book is available from the British Library.

Penn Cottage Books
P.O. Box 121
Chorley
PR6 8GF
Tel: 01257 260347

tage Books, Penn Cottage, PO
ashire, England PR6 8GF
ww.verawaters.com

Parts of this book have previously been published in Vera Waters' first two books, **Half a Rainbow** and **The Other Half of the Rainbow** (both now out of print) and have been included here to fit in with what the author is trying to achieve.

Printed and bound by Beacon DM Ltd, West Yorks.
(Tel: 01535 680381)

Cover design by Freebird Media Ltd
www.freebird.co.uk

Illustrations by Ron Whittaker and Leonard Varley

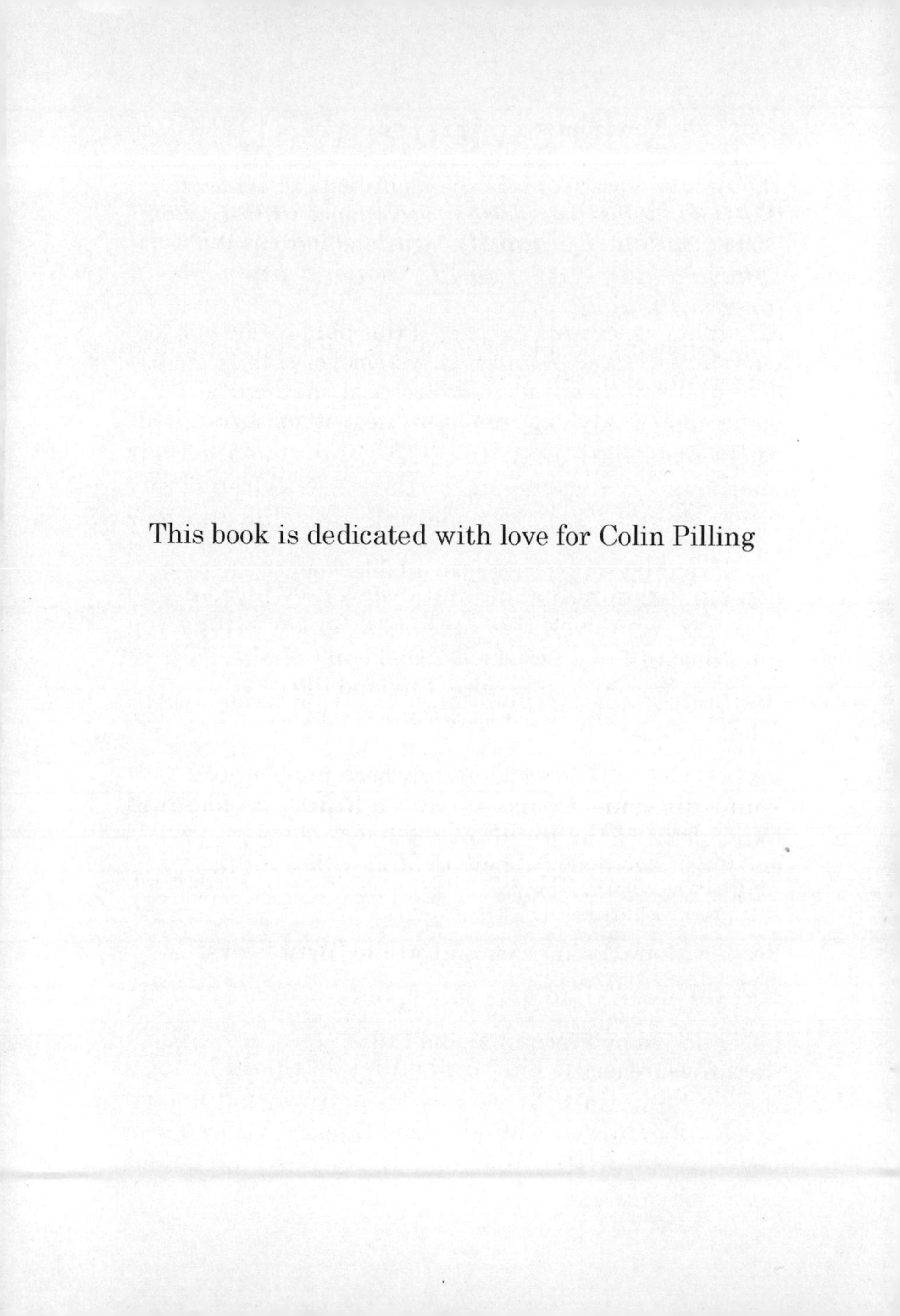

This book is dedicated with love for Colin Pilling

Acknowledgments

Whilst writing this book I have been surrounded by family and friends without whose help it would never have been accomplished.

The following people have all played a part and are deserving of my thanks.

Nick, Jon and Izzy, my children, who throughout their lives have been the 'the wind beneath their mother's wings'; and their children, my grandchildren, who I hope will take life in their stride.

Nick, for reminding me that everyone who comes to see me, whatever the reason, is given strong tea and biscuits!

Bethany, my granddaughter, for the cover photograph.

Colin, my son-in-law, for his jokes and banter, now suddenly gone from us leaving a huge void in all our lives.

Jeanne, always simply 'there' for me, and Michael, my good friends.

Sister Mary John, my mentor for thirty years.

Dr. Clive Barker, for his empathy and understanding.

Some years ago whilst on holiday in Spain I met a lovely lady; Kath. It was as though we had known each other forever. When the time came for us to say goodbye she handed me a slip of paper requesting that I read it later. I did. It said 'if ever you need a place to lay your head to rest and be loved come to me at this address'. I did as she requested, and we spent such happy times together until last December when she died.

John Gammons, my literary agent, for his support, patience and advice.

Dee, my secretary, for her help and Catherine who, at the last minute gave CD expertise.

Freebird Media for the cover design.

Illustrators Leonard Varley and Ron Whittaker, both talented artists.

This list would be incomplete without mention of the encouragement and hospitality I have received from across the pond particularly from my friends Phyl & Joe in Virginia, Scott &, Bobbi in Chicago, Johnne & Linda Iowa, Rick and Bob, Patsy and Laurie, Julie, Erik & Trina to name but a few.........

I have felt humbled throughout my life that the people who seek my help not only give me their trust but in so doing enlist me as the custodian of the secrets of their very souls.
Each and everyone of those people are acknowledged here and I thank them individually for that privilege and the permission to share their true stories and experiences in the hope that it will encourage and inspire others.

Vera Waters

Contents

Introduction - Just to say

If I were there with you in person, as you read these first few words, I would in all probability offer you a cup of tea. If you said you preferred coffee I would hesitate as I know that I cannot make a good cup of coffee for the life of me! Choose tea and you are all right, it will be strong and yes it will be served with jam and cream biscuits, or maybe shortbreads.

You see, it is one of my rituals, a habit, something that I do. What would we speak of, you and I, as we shared a hot drink? Would you tell me of your life and how you feel? Maybe you would be quiet and contemplative, who knows?

All the tales and stories told here are true. They are about people, interesting people who I have met or seen from a distance. The stories are about ordinary situations, everyday life at home and abroad. We pass strangers in the street, crossing the road, walking the dog, driving the car, sitting on a park bench, all of them people who have their own lives of which we know nothing. They are passing strangers.

At this moment you and I are meeting through these pages, and so I bid you welcome in the hope and belief that as you read you will find that what I have written gives you food for thought.

If a tear finds it way down your cheek, or if you find yourself saying 'I have done that', or are reminded of someone you love, if you smile or laugh as you read then be assured that was my intention, and if you feel comforted, challenged or simply relaxed then I am pleased.

A famous author once said that when each of her books was finished she felt as though she had given birth. In some way I agree, but it is the reader who gives something new to the world if, having read, they feel inspired.

We can be sure of nothing but the moment in which we stand.
Get the very best out of your life.
You have a lot to give!

Vera Waters

Emotional Banking

I plunged my hands into the hot sudsy water, almost up to my elbows and as the warmth travelled up my arms the memories came flooding into my head. Hand washing is one of my 'fight the blues' remedies. Instead of piling the 'whites' into my more than adequate washing machine I decide that I need my therapy...I've been doing it for years. So as I stood beside the sink looking through my kitchen window my mind made a journey into another place, another kitchen sink in yet another lifetime.

During my professional life many caring people have shown their empathy for me by asking 'who counsels the counsellor?'
When the question comes from someone in a large audience it is often difficult to explain where I find strength and support. After I have explained that I have a loving family, together with a strong belief in my maker, I pass on to respond to other raised hands in the group.
If the same question is asked in a more intimate setting then I feel that I can elaborate by telling them about my emotional banking system and how it works.

When people come to me as a life coach I try to explain that we all need to be able to find our own inner peace. Often they reply with 'Oh, I'm not religious'. This always makes me smile as I say

'neither am I'. At this they often heave a sigh of obvious relief, then we both smile.
There is such a difference between being 'religious' and being 'spiritual'. To lead more fulfilling lives we have to not only link into our mind and body but also our spirit. A firm belief in a greater being than ourselves can be of enormous help and support and my beliefs are a great help to me. Many people who lack such a faith find it difficult to link with the spirit within, often peace eludes them.

We need help to link into our inner self. Nature often provides that help. Earlier today a friend and I took my dog for a walk in the woods close to her house. It has been a crisp sunny day after the hard frost of last night. Jess, my soft hearted faithful labrador bounded around, returning with one stick after another and finally with part of a heavy branch. As my friend and I laughed together at these canine antics we heard a sound that quieted us immediately.
'Is that a woodpecker?'
'It can't be a woodpecker'.
'It *is* a woodpecker, there it goes again'.
'But it's only January'.
We stood transfixed, silent for a while. We tried to locate the bird and saw a blurred feathery shape high up on the trunk of a very tall tree.
'Wish I'd brought my binoculars' said my companion.
'I wish you'd brought your binoculars' I replied and we both laughed.

Jess, although previously unwilling to relinquish her hold on the stick of her choice suddenly, claiming our attention, dropped it at my feet. Her eyes said 'throw, I want to run' but we two friends were unwilling to break the spell, the magic of the moment, we had heard a woodpecker, busy, in a tree.

Afterwards, enjoying cups of tea, we remarked how lucky we are to live close to the countryside. Now I'm suggesting that woodpeckers and hand washing have a lot in common, at least for me because both experiences make deposits in my emotional bank. If we are to feel more fulfilled during our time in this world our emotional banking system needs maintaining every day of our lives.

Imagine a new born baby, a child whose arrival brings a smile to the faces of everyone in the family. The 'baby shower' with so many presents, the proud parents and relatives surrounded by the love of friends and family.
That is when the emotional banking system starts. Right there and then, with the first gulp of air that we take as we enter this world. The account is set up with a huge deposit; the love of our parents. These deposits continue as each day passes, the cuddles, the cooing, the baby talk, those first sounds and actions that the little one experiences in his or her life. One deposit after another; a brilliant start to a life and soon a healthy balance in this most important of banking systems. That is if you are lucky.

Many of the people we meet in our lives have not had such beneficial experiences and consequently they have a different tale to tell. To be born into a world without love is bad enough, but what of those children who soon learn that their parents offer only a brief shadow of the love all of us need. For those individuals the emotional bank is very soon out of credit, so sad. I particularly the like the quotation 'what does not kill us strengthens us'. Often we read of people who have achieved greatness, who began life with nothing in the way of emotional deposits; and what of those people who have experienced great suffering or trauma, experience that has made such a huge withdrawal from their emotional bank that it is difficult for them to recover; but recover they do, despite everything.
Keeping a good balance in our emotional bank is our responsibility. It's no use expecting other people to be there to top up the balance for you. As President Truman said 'The buck stops here'.
As our emotional bank is of such importance to our wellbeing we should know how to make those deposits. Many people deep down inside know that they neglect the deposits, whilst others have no idea what I am talking about.

To give you a little food for thought consider the following.

Some years ago on a mid November evening I closed the door of my office in St John's Street, Manchester to walk to the car park. It was dark and cold. I remember wishing that I had left earlier. I did not have far to walk but never the less I hurried, wanting to be at home, warm and snug. As I drew near to the car park something rolled across the pavement in front of my feet. Looking down I saw a large, shiny, brown conker. Bending down I picked it up only to find myself rubbing specks of dirt off its surface. Looking around I realised that there was not a tree in sight; just empty pavements, cold, hard, impersonal but practical pavements. Where could it have come from, some one had obviously dropped it? Possibly a small boy perhaps visiting the city, a boy from the suburbs, a boy who collected conkers and kept at least one in his pocket.

It was the end of a hard day for me, a day of counselling police officers, all of whom were suffering as a result of serious attacks during the course of their work. My emotional bank was heavy on the withdrawal side. Yes, we professionals are supposed to have 'off switches' but as far as I am concerned the day that switch stays permanently in the 'off' position I need to stop what I do.
Finding that simple natural evidence of life placed a huge deposit in my bank; a smile to my face and gave me a feeling of hope.

Sometime later I mentioned it to a business acquaintance, describing how I had felt, how I had wondered at how the conker could have found its way onto the busy city street.

His reply 'It was only a conker,Vera, all that fuss over a conker!' Thank goodness he was a colleague and not a friend!

We find our deposits for the emotional bank in different places, at different times; varied experiences colour our lives. However, when reviewing your emotional bank try giving the following a little time and thought, you could well be surprised at your answers...

When did you last walk along a beach with someone you love?

Did you scuff your feet in the leaves last autumn?

When did you last watch the sun rise?

Has a child taken your hand in theirs recently?

Have you laughed lately?

When did you praise someone and say 'well done'?

Were the stars out last night or didn't you notice?

Is it an age since you listened to the sound of the sea; looked in awe at a mountain or simply paddled in a brook?

As a parent how often do you let your children know that you love them no matter what age they are?

Do you like rainbows?

How often do you dance or sing?

Do you love your pet as much as your pet loves you?

If this list gives you food for thought then simply note that if you are planning to do all or, indeed, any of these things at a later date when there is a space in your busy life, remember that you may only have today!

Hand washing gives me a deposit because I have such lovely memories of doing this simple chore when my children were small. I am reminded of the time when, married for a few years, we still could not afford to buy the then fashionable twin tub washer. We were struggling. With a two year old and a newborn baby I could not return to teaching. At that time six weeks maternity leave was the maximum. Life was hard in some ways, living in a tiny cottage in the country but for me washday was a joy.

After boiling the water I would put the clothes to soak, then when the water was hand hot I would push the garments through the suds with my hands. Much later, as the water cooled, my two year old son would help me and we would blow the bubbles from our fingers whilst his baby brother slept peacefully in the Moses basket beside us. Such happy times.

All my life this simple practice has helped to keep me sane. It is one of my rituals; a symbol of peace and hope. Most of my professional life I have been 'on-call', often for twenty four hours, day in day out. The telephone would ring and I would be alert, ready to deal with the next call out. It was necessary to find strategies, ways to compensate for all the pain and suffering I saw and heard. Every client who came to me for help left with a tiny part of me in their pocket. The parts I gave away had to be re-grown as deposits in my emotional bank.

Every year when autumn arrives I find myself out in the woods with some of my grandchildren collecting conkers. Truth to tell, when they are not around I collect conkers, with the dog of course. Do you know why? It's because I can't guarantee that I will be around to collect them next year. This is not a maudlin thought, it is quite positive really because I want to live every minute of my life and so I believe should you.
My conkers gathering places another deposit in the bank as does every rainbow that I see. Rainbows are wonderful, coming as they do midst rain and sunshine. Scientific explanations leave me cold as they rob the experience of its spontaneous magic. The rainbow is very special, a gift of colour and the suggestion of something intangible yet full of promise!

Everyone has a different list; we are all individuals, this is what makes us so unique; the practice of emotional banking will change your life, as a consequence you will have a greater, deeper feeling of well-being.

The warmth of the sudsy water, the washing of the garments, and the return of the good memories... already I feel better!

Friendship

Friendship is love. Friendship enriches our lives and makes life's passage easier. The love of a friend is invaluable. True friendship cannot be bought, coerced or diminished. Good friends function out of a loving union, links in a chain, friend to friend, trust to trust. Patience to patience, tolerance to even more tolerance and so the friendship grows.

A good friend is one who you call in the night saying "please come, please come," "I am on my way" replies the friend. No enquiry, no questions — "what do you want? what is the matter?" simply "I am coming to be with you whatever the problem."

A true friend, woman to woman, notices the bags under your eyes, the dark patches almost hidden by clever makeup. A true friend man to man notices that you are less tolerant, that you are smoking and drinking more than usual. A true friend knows when there is a tiredness in your voice and a very good and close friend telephones you just as you are about to make the call yourself.

A friend knows the colours you prefer, the food you like to eat, your pet hates and fears, whilst the truest of all friends bathes in your reflected glory as you receive recognition for an action or work well done. This is indeed true friendship without envy, jealousy or petulance, a relationship based on love. What kind of a friend are you?

God gave us our relatives;
Thank God we can choose
our friends

Ethel Watts Mumford

In life most of us need positive friendships, however friendships that become weighty sometimes become extremely strained. Very recently I strained a friendship considerably. Things were happening in my life that were hurting me a great deal. I became blind to the needs of a very dear friend. His needs were not my concern, because in my need of him I wanted his response and his support, so that he could help me. I was moaning and bewailing a situation which, in fact, I could not change and during this period I missed his birthday. I had never, ever, missed his birthday, and I have known him for 20 years, but this year I did. You see I didn't really share, I was too busy taking from the friendship.

When working I found that I was able to switch off that negative part of my personality, but when I met with this good and trusted friend, when he hugged me and helped me, I loaded him up with the weight of my problems.

Eventually, he grew tired of saying "it can't be changed, you are losing your peace of mind." Then I became angry with him, because I felt that there should be more to the situation than there was. I wanted him to offer solutions which he could not do. And so we came to a situation in which he grew tired of my constant taking, so much so that for a brief time he absented himself from my life. It was only then, when he was no longer there to call upon, that I looked in on my own selfishness. It's so easy to say to friends they should be able to give or take whatever we need, but even friendship has its limitations because it requires us to 'work at it' just like any other relationship. It is about give and take, and sadly, in this situation, all I was doing was taking.

What are your friendships like? When did you last look at them? When did you last measure how much you give and how much take? A week, a month, a year, is it so long since you evaluated what friendship is really about? It's so easy to become someone who is seen to be a very sound and stable individual, but who privately needs a great deal of support and help. We can lean on our friends but that leaning can become so burdensome to the trusted friend, that eventually, they, in their weariness, creep away, or even worse, start to avoid us in subtle ways that we cannot quite measure. The friend may stoically continue to give support until one day, bursting at the seams, they say "for goodness sake, when did you last think of me?" Then we are brought rapidly to a halt, and in the mirror, should we care to look, we would see the reflection of our own selfishness.

Friendship is about trusting and it is true, as George Eliot said, that we should not have a need to weigh words but friendship is about the balance between giving and taking. It matters so much that an imbalance does not readily occur. Sometimes a group of people working together in a shop, an office, a bank, a hospital, may get on very well. Daily they exchange chat and gossip. Some of them have particular friendships within the group. Within that group is someone who talks so much about his or her problems, that the group eventually becomes tired and the topic of conversation between the other members is about how they cannot cope with the 'taking' of the one other person. How sad, I wonder if any member of that group is kind enough, and understanding enough, to talk to that person about what he or she is doing. How can we learn if we do not have guidance?

How about stopping now and thinking about your friends. Now is the time to invite that special friend round for a meal. What about that friend who lives quite a way from you, who was so good when you needed them two years ago? When did you last speak on the phone, when did you last send a letter? It is too late when our friends are no longer there to share with. Remember that the other person in the equation could have as many misgivings as you yourself. That person could need your reassurance.

A good way to ease the burden of your lack of confidence is to try to imagine that other people can feel exactly as underconfident as you. Friendship is born out of need. A need for support, help and comfort. Friendships are often formed between people with similar likes, dislikes and interests. It is a way of expressing our needs whilst at the same time we meet the needs of others.

However in order to love others and to attract the love of others into ourselves we first need to value the person we really are. To measure our own talents and gifts! Although we may presume we have little or nothing to offer in terms of friendship there will be something within our personality that can become attractive to others.

When something happens in your life that leaves

you feeling very unhappy it often helps to talk it through with a trusted friend. The sharing of the burden usually causes the sympathetic reaction you need at that time. The sharing helps you to feel comforted. However, as time passes the unhappy experience needs to move from your present into your recent past and hopefully after the passage of further time into the far past. All these stages take time. Often returning to the original friend who still constantly refers to the experience will only serve to keep you in a negative frame of mind. Hindering you when you have decided to feel much more positive.

How often have you felt indebted to a friend who has listened? A person who when you were low gave you support. Remembering that, that same friend cannot necessarily be blamed when he or she refers back to the shared confidence. When we confide our innermost secrets to our friends we actually bear not only our souls but we open our wounds. Avoiding the friend often does not work, only leading to a situation in which there is mistrust and great misunderstanding. Both parties then feel uneasy and unsure of the original friendship.

Why not give your friendship some guidelines? Carefully explain that you found their help at the time of the crisis absolutely invaluable, that you need their help to continue but in a different way because without them you would find it difficult to put the past behind you and get on with your life. A good friend will be understanding and do as you ask.

When you know that you are feeling negative remember that at that time there will be constant withdrawals from your emotional bank. This is not the time to go to see the relative who always has something to moan about. Make the decision to steer clear of those people who will make you feel negative and miserable. Just because at some time they may have listened to you moaning and groaning about life, doesn't give them the right to expect you to do the same at the drop of a hat.

The next time you decide to talk to a friend or relative about your innermost secrets try to remember that the timing of these disclosures can matter a great deal. Before dropping all of your pain on the shoulders of another person try to remember to look at their eyes. Ask yourself "can they take this?" Already by that very thought process, by thinking about another person you are beginning to think positive rather than negative. Because you put the feelings of another person before yourself you help the process to continue.

Surely in this day and age with the celebration of Father's and Mother's Days to say nothing of non smoking days etc, I am sure that someone should have thought of inventing a Friend's Day. If they have, I have not heard of it. However, instead of it being a commercial venture, it should be personal. Tomorrow needs to be the day that you make into a Friend's Day for you! We need our friends, we need our relatives, but often our friends get closer to us than those to whom we are related.

Trusting a friend
is like opening a box and
liking what you find inside

Vera Waters

Had I the heavens embroidered cloths,
Enwrought with golden and silver light,
The blue and the dim and the dark cloths
Of night and light and the half-light

I would spread the cloths under your feet:
But I being poor, have only my dreams:
I have spread my dreams under your feet;
Tread softly because you tread upon my dreams

William Butler Yeats

The Kindness Curve

Acts of kindness ensure that life is made more pleasant and more enjoyable. Often we remember them for a lifetime. Who cannot fail to recall some small act of kindness from the past? Travel back, reach into your memories, there will be something there to recall. Kindness is packaged in many ways, often in very small acts that reassure us that another person cares.

For some of us, kindness comes naturally, for others this is not so. If you have never received kindness it is so easy to become bitter and closed to what kindness can mean in your life. My home is filled with knick-knacks, trinkets, most of which I did not buy or choose myself. Some of them I would never have chosen as they are not to my taste and yet I value them immensely. These items are tangible proof of the kindness of other people. One is a glass rainbow, well half a rainbow to be exact. It was made by a young professional woman who came to see me during what she described as a 'bad patch' in her life. I suggested that she take up a new hobby, attend a course, meet people through whom she could gain reassurance that she was worth something, that she had talents and gifts unique to her. It took a great deal of effort for her to join the glass making group but she did it and then presented me with one of her first successes. She made the time and put in the effort to create something especially for me to celebrate the title of

my first book. How hard it must have been for her to give away one of the first examples of her new found creative talent.
Another gift is an oddly shaped piece of wood, given to me as I left Australia to remind me, the giver said, of down under. 'Don't you ever forget being here and come back soon.'

And then there are the teddies. No, I do not collect teddy bears, I have never collected these friendly furry toys and yet I have in my possession hundreds of them. They look at me from every corner of my house.
Why? Well, it all began with a simple act of kindness.
During my years counselling police officers I met people who had been badly assaulted or injured. Long after their physical wounds had healed they continued to carry the emotional burden of the inner scars that take so much longer to heal. One such officer struggled to come to terms with his assault. Attacked from behind he didn't see his assailant. The fact that his attacker had not been apprehended meant that he could not store the experience away in his mind, in today's terms he did not have closure on the experience; he was left with unfinished business.
The day arrived when he was declared fit to resume his duties, not so easy after months of sick leave. Weeks later he telephoned my secretary for an appointment, saying that he wouldn't keep me for long. Fearing the worst I wondered if he had returned to his duties too early and that maybe he had needed longer to recover. I need not have

worried, When he arrived he was carrying a brightly coloured gift bag.

'I just came back to let you know that we found the men who attacked me. There were four of them. I didn't stand a chance. Even if I hadn't been knocked unconscious, I couldn't have done much. The relief in his face was tangible. He was actually telling me that he felt that he had not failed after all. The fact that there was more than one attacker meant that he could reassure himself that he had performed his duties as a police officer to the best of his ability.

'Thanks for helping me. Oh, and I brought you this.' He handed me the bag, inside was a big box of chocolates but underneath a layer of pink tissue paper was a beautiful dark brown teddy bear. 'He's jointed' said my client. 'My wife thought you might like him, to remind you how we appreciate what you have done for me.'

With that, looking very embarrassed, he hurriedly kissed me on the cheek before he went out of the door.

I left the bag with the teddy on a shelf beside my desk but because I am so sentimental I placed the teddy with his head sticking out at the top. Well he looked so cheerful and seemed to brighten up the room.

Two weeks later, another officer seeing me for his last appointment, presented me with a big cuddly yellow teddy. 'I thought you might like this' he said, going very red in the face. 'I know you like them, you had one here in a bag on that book case

the last time I came, he reminded me of my children. I told my wife when she came to pick me up, so now he has a mate. We got you a different colour as Jane said when she was little she had a yellow one that she took everywhere with her. Our daughter has a white one it's forever hanging out on the washing line, doesn't keep clean for long'.
He hadn't meant to say so much I know, giving me such insights into his family. Another kiss on the cheek as he left and another teddy bear for me..

That was how the teddy bear collection began, all part of the kindness curve, word spread. Police officers and their wives gave me teddy bears because they 'knew' that I liked them! The word spread, imagine my surprise when a group of nurses after one of my training courses gave me a lovely bear.
'A little bird told us that you have a passion for bears' they said smiling. Then a group of managers in the corporate world presented me with a bear, doctors, soldiers, housewives, carers, parents whenever I met people in training, presentations or as individual clients the bears arrived.

Very soon they numbered thirty, then fifty, and all too soon one hundred bears needed some place to live. Multiply that by a career of over thirty years and you can imagine and appreciate that there were times when some of the original teddies looked pretty grim at being usurped by so many newcomers and I gave up looking for spaces in which they could be housed.
Did it end there? Not a bit of it! My family joined in too. Small grandchildren come armed with

teddies because 'grandma likes them!' Somehow I became caught up in the whole 'teddy bear' business even rescuing forlorn looking bears from the windows of charity shops.

Suddenly I remembered what I had always believed that everything that happens in our lives happens for a purpose. I thought of a way to bring smiles to the faces of the little children who came to see me needing help.
Many of them had suffered so much that they had become mute. They spoke to no one because to speak would be too risky, too painful. These children had been hurt by adults who should have loved them. They were victims of injustice and cruelty, children whose faith in people was so shattered and fragmented that many experts they had seen came to the conclusion that they might never recover. Often I felt that when all else had failed these little precious people were referred to me or brought by despairing parents who felt that the care systems available to them had failed miserably. .
I began by placing a selection of my teddies in the room so that when the children came to see me they would see these furry creatures and hopefully respond in some way.
One day a little boy came to see me. He was five years old; he didn't want to speak; in fact he hadn't spoken for quite a time. He wasn't aggressive, he wasn't nasty, he simply sat and looked and said nothing. He was incredibly sad. Reading through the notes on what had happened to him during his short life I knew that no one could blame him for

not wanting to speak. Why should he, there was not one person he could possibly trust, every adult who had promised to be close to him had let him down. That was something he felt sure about; grown ups let you down! He knew that for certain. I could see it in his face.

He came to see me with his grandmother, a woman who was trying valiantly in the autumn of her life to make up for the wrongs he had suffered. She was loving and kind and totally worn out. She had taken him to specialists and consultants all without success. It was to emerge later that her grandson thought that because she had grey hair she was old and therefore would die soon and he would be alone again. Another adult that he loved gone!
I picked up one of the teddies from the chair in my office. Sitting on the floor at the little boy's feet I told him the story of the bear; how I had seen him at a rummage sale and knew instinctively that no one would buy him because he had only one arm. The other was gone. I explained how I had felt when I saw him; that I couldn't leave him there, an injured bear, an unwanted bear, I had to take him home.

Every word I said was true. That was exactly how I had felt that day at the rummage sale.
The child listened as I explained how the other bears came into my life, of the big strong policemen who came for help.
In complete silence he took the bear, and then placed his face on the woolly cheek of the toy. He tentatively felt the place where the missing arm

should have been and then he gently cuddled his new found friend.
'Would you care for him' I said 'he needs special love, just for himself. I think he would like to go home with you, that is if you could be very gentle with him. You see he is rather scared at the moment, have you room for him in your heart' I placed my hand where my heart is as I said this. The little boy looked at the bear and with his right hand touched his chest.
A silent tear found its way down his grandmother's cheek; we smiled together. 'Strong tea and a biscuit?' I asked, she nodded.
We sat hugging mugs of tea whilst the little one sipped a cold drink still holding onto teddy.
Several sessions later this little boy would come in and rearrange the other teddies on the chair in my office, having of course first placed his by then much loved friend in the protective arms of his grandmother.

Obviously when he eventually decided that it was safe enough to speak he spoke to his teddy first which was hardly surprising.
Now I am not suggesting that the therapy was instantly successful. It wasn't, it took months of hard work by the three of us but that one armed teddy bear opened a door into this small boy's misery and despair.
The kindness curve, this little boy, so damaged, so misused, was capable of feeling kindness for a small teddy bear without an arm.

He could empathise but I was reminded that without the thoughtful kindness of my adult clients I would not have had a collection of teddies in the first place.
These police officers and their wives or girlfriends, the nurses who sought my help, the doctors finding it hard to cope with long hours and little rest would never know until now how much their kind gifts helped others. That is how kindness works, a single act of kindness can reverberate in ways we may never know.

There was an occasion when I was asked to spend some time with a group of 'high powered' business men. The owners of the company for which they worked wanted them to work together more ably as a team.
In order to achieve this I set up a residential course at my training centre in Scotland.
We worked our way through many soul searching hours and still one man insisted that he did not make mistakes in work situations, and that because of his vast experience he was rarely if ever wrong. His colleagues tried to reason with him, suggesting that he prevented the team from working in harmony but he would have none of it.
After 'lights out' each evening his co-managers would knock at my door almost begging me to bring him to his senses. Of course, we must now all behave in a politically correct sense; it is doubtful that during my work I have subscribed to some of the more restrictive areas of this so called correctness, so having thought through the problem with the group I arrived at a possible solution.

The next day I carried a brown teddy bear into the group. I placed him beside my chair so that everyone could see him and then simply continued as usual with the exercise. We were discussing motivation and how we can motivate each other. Eventually Ron, a good humoured member of the group, began to smile and then to laugh. 'I am sorry' he said 'but it's the bear, is he going to join in?'

At this everyone, with the exception of Mr 'Always Right' began at first to smile and then to laugh. A fit of giggles overtook the group. The positive jollity was shattered into a thousand pieces by the next words spoken. Their colleague told them all to be quiet, to stop laughing.
'Do you know how stupid you look? She's making fools of you'. With that he stood up.
'Please wait' I said, 'come, sit down and let us look at what is really happening here. After much persuasion from us all he did eventually rejoin the group and sat down.
'It isn't a trick. It is simply a brown bear, usually he lives with all the others either in my office or at home. I told them where the bears came from, how the collection started. It was then that I decided to take the group on a journey, to tell them a true story about a teddy bear.

I explained how a police officer who had been very badly injured whilst working had been given a bear by his small son. The officer had cried on receiving the gift.
'Daddy' his son had said, 'it is alright 'cos my bear will make you better.' That man was over six foot

and built like a brick wall but a small boy believed that his teddy bear could bring about the required miracle.

'When I brought this bear into the room I was hoping that he would also work a miracle.' As I said this I looked at the man who constantly believed he could not make a mistake. 'We all needed a miracle to help us to realize that there is no skill or talent in being the 'inhibiting factor' in any group or family. You are of value here and in the workplace but just like the bear we all need to be liked and loved. This bear is a gift of kindness to you' and with that I handed him the brown bear.

'Keep him' I said.

There was a stunned silence, then I realized that there were tears in his eyes. The woman to his right silently put out her hand, he hesitated and then passed the toy to her.

'He's for you' she said, pushing the bear back towards him. 'Work with us Tom. Not against us.'

Tom kept the bear.

A few weeks after the course ended Tom came to see me, to tell me how he felt about the whole experience. He said that he couldn't wait to share his experience with his wife later in the week on his return home.

'She listened and then she hugged me and cried saying 'Oh Tom you don't have to be right all the time. I love you even when you are wrong and have got the wrong end of the stick completely'.

Before he left me he said 'I just need to pop out to the car. I've brought you something, a present'.

Yes, you've guessed, it was a grey bear with jointed arms and legs 'To add to your collection'.
For years each Christmas a card would arrive, not really a festive card although it came to wish me the season's greetings. I always knew it was from him; there was a grey bear on the front.
Tom had experienced kindness from his management colleagues during the course, from his wife on his return home and through a simple toy, a teddy bear, and also I hope from me.

It is easy for the sceptics to dismiss kindness as though it is nothing at all. However to underestimate the power of kindness is to deny yourself the benefits of its gifts and in so doing also probably deprive others of its powerful ongoing, far reaching impact.
Kindness has to start somewhere, the small acts begin with you. Imagine making kindness an integral part of your life, an everyday action, a reflection of who you are and what you do. Children that grow up in a kind, giving environment learn to be kind at an early age. The actions you may take for granted, the small things that you do everyday and have never seen as powerful ARE powerful.
You can change things around you, you can be part of the kindness curve of life if you choose to 'join up!'

Everyone has a Story to Tell

People who make an impact on our lives are often those we find interesting; people who within a few moments have captured our attention.

We want to listen to them; they strike a chord within us, and very soon we find ourselves being transported into other realms of thought. These people are the storytellers, they have tales to tell, events to report, circumstances to describe.

Those who aspire to public speaking may well seek expertise from special courses or lessons but the true storyteller is aware that to tell a story well you must first have the capacity to listen. Not all those who speak in public are good listeners but it is soon easy to see the real narrator as he or she stands out in a crowd.

Since time began we have told each other stories, reported on what we have seen, where we have been and who we met on that part of our journey through life. In fact every single thing that we do is part of a story, it is the story of how we feel, how we react to any given situation. Our story is unique, it is our own, others may have similar experiences but the way we see life is special to us. Everyone we meet has a different script, another life, their life.

We relate to stories, we form images in our mind as the teller speaks. These mind pictures are our own, private, special, just for us; our very own unique perception as we visualise. Through the narrators descriptive words we are invited to enter in! The art of storytelling is as old as life itself and just as meaningful. Every person creates a different image as they listen to what we have to say. There are stories from the present; daily happenings; there are stories from the past, each story taking the listener on a journey. We can lose ourselves in another world; in a tale, a legend, even a myth.

Looking back we can see our life events, the circumstances, the people we met, those we knew at that time, often remembering with great clarity a room, the furniture, so many details. These are our stories. They helped us to develop into the people we are now.

Here is a story that began in the late forties. It is a true story to take you on a journey into another life.

......

The first thing I noticed about the small room was the draining board. It was old, worn, wet from a recent scrubbing, next to it a white sink, snow white; everything was so clean. I stood beside Sister Gabriel holding on to the heavy basket. She was a teacher at the convent school that I attended. At that time when members of religious orders went out from the convent into the community they had to be accompanied. It was not permissible for them to travel alone. Good catholic man that he was my father volunteered my services. The minimum age for this much sought after, prestigious work was nine years, so as soon as I chronologically qualified I was set the task. Every Saturday from nine in the morning until three in the afternoon I accompanied Sister Gabriel on her 'charitable works' as they were called. On rare occasions I would be asked to take her on the bus into Manchester to visit the Mother house, a much bigger convent where I sat on a very uncomfortable chair in the great hall whilst she went to meet with the other sisters.

The day I walked into that kitchen was a Saturday in mid-summer. The house was situated at the edge of a large council housing estate; the garden was trim and the doorstep, like the sink, sparkling white.
That day I was particularly happy because the nun whom I accompanied was my favourite of them all. The headmistress of my school, no less, but as she told me in later years her position and learning counted for nothing in the pecking order of convent life! As we set out that morning she had told me that I would recognize the people in some of the houses we visited but that I was to tell no one of the purpose of her visit to them. Each of us carried a basket, mine smaller than hers. I was thankful for her thoughtfulness as the unknown contents were very heavy, making the carrying of it very difficult. On the way we had stopped several times for me to rest. I loved this woman who, unlike her 'Sisters', bent beside me and made sure that I was alright...'nearly there child, nearly there'.

We knocked at the door, a woman with a shiny red face opened it. 'Good morning Sister, come in; will you sit down? Shall I lift the basket onto the table for you?'

My adult companion nodded, 'Thank you Alice, the wee one could do with a drink of Adam's ale I think, she is nearly out on her feet.' They both looked at me kindly.

Quaffing the water in a quite unladylike way I noticed there were two girls standing in the doorway. I knew one of them quite well as she was in my class at school; her name was Barbara. Her younger sister was in the reception class and had only started school the year previously.

'Shall we take the things out now?' The question was not directed at me and I watched as Sister lifted the cloths that covered the contents of the heavy baskets, placing on the table jam and cheese, bread which was obviously homemade, margarine and what looked like dripping in a cracked old basin. There were other grocery items that surprised me as it was still a time of rationing and finding provisions was hard in those post-war years. My basket surrendered a big brown paper bag marked flour and at the bottom some clothes...'for the baby, we need to be getting you ready'. It was only then that I noticed how fat Mrs Hebden was, she was having a baby!

The two girls did not move from the doorway. They simply stared.
Sister went over to them and stroked their hair 'it is alright, don't worry, Vera won't say anything. She knows that it is an honour to be given the job of accompanying me; she knows the rules!'
The older girl looked doubtful. I went to her and smiled.
'I won't say anything.' I whispered.

As we walked back to the convent Sister explained to me that there could be problems for the girls if other children in school discovered that they were on the 'Charity 'list. 'Their father is away and cannot support his family and with a new baby due in a few weeks they need all the help they can get. 'Vera, children can be very cruel, so not a word'. She placed a finger to her lips.

Looking back I ask myself why the scrubbed draining board made such an impact on me. Our house was spotless too, but perhaps it was because there was little evidence of possessions or money in their house. This was so true, as I discovered during the many visits that followed. Whilst mine was full of beautiful furniture that was considered to be so grand that it had to be covered by dustsheets the whole time, theirs was shabby but clean. They had so little!

On a much later visit I was not surprised to find Barbara wearing the 'Milly Molly Mandy' dress that my mother had made for me the previous year which, after numerous hem droppings, was now too small for me. On that occasion Barbara said 'Mum doesn't let me wear it for school cos people would know, so I wear it at weekends.' She fingered the green and pink gingham material 'Vera, you do have some lovely dresses' she said.

The girls believed that their father was away looking for work. He had been a soldier fighting in the war, but try as he might he could not find work at all. It was easy for them to accept the explanation given by their mother for their father's prolonged absence. They felt sorry for him, far away in another part of the country, knocking on doors, asking to be given a paid job. They listened and believed their mother's story.

Just as I was about to leave primary school to go to the grammar school convent in the city something happened that changed my life and the lives of those two girls who as the months passed had become my dear friends.

One day a whispered warning was passed between the girls and boys in my class, but when the message got to me it stopped short. I was left out of the loop. Inside I was gripped with anxiety and fear. I had experienced this only a couple of times before but on both occasions it had signalled a violent happening. I could see that Barbara was not given the message either.
A boy sitting behind me touched my shoulder, 'be careful Vera' he whispered.

After class I walked towards the school gates with Barbara after collecting her younger sister, who was patiently waiting outside the door to the infants' class. A group of children from our class, girls and boys we knew, our classmates with whom we played every day, were waiting just beyond the school gates. I could feel the fear rising inside me. Violence of any sort made me want to cry. Barbara took hold of my hand and put her other arm around her sister in a protective way.
'What do they want?' I asked.
'Don't know' replied my friend, 'but I'm scared!'
That made three of us.
We stopped beside the gate as the group of children began to shout at us. At first I thought that their abuse was to be shared by all three of us, then I realised that their viscious taunts were not directed at me but the other two girls standing beside me. I gripped Barbara's hand more tightly than ever.

The ring leader stepped forward. Her name was Bernadette and she lived close to Barbara's house. 'Your dad's not looking for work, ee's in prison. Ee's a dirty man, my dad says he should be hung for what he did to those children in Newcastle' and with that she picked up a stone and hurled it towards us. The others soon followed suit, whilst Barbara and I tried to protect her little sister. We backed our way to the school buildings to be met by the welcome sound of the school caretaker who thankfully had heard the noise and decided to investigate.

'Hoy you lot, get off 'ome before I go across to the convent and get the Sisters.'

Bernadette stepped closer to the gate, glaring at our rescuer. 'My dad says you can't get a proper job cos you're not all there in the 'ead.' She tapped her forehead in a meaningful way. But Bernadette could not see what the rest of us could see so clearly. Coming up behind her at a smart trot was our headmistress, she of the baskets and the Saturday visits no less. Hearing the commotion she had taken a different route to the school gates so that now she stood directly behind the band of bullies. She placed her hand firmly on Bernadette's shoulders. 'And what would your father know about anything?' she asked. The colour drained from the girl's face but, quickly recovering herself, she said 'It's true Sister, their dad is in prison for what he did; 'ees a filthy man'. In those times being politically correct was not part of the equation. Sister Gabriel, never known for violent outbursts, unlike so many of the other nuns, grabbed the shouting girl by the shoulders of her jacket. She appeared to rise from the ground, only to find herself roughly deposited a few feet away.

'Tomorrow, your father and mother will report to my office at nine sharp. Go home, give them the message and explain to them why they have to come. Do I make myself clear?'

The girl turned and this time we could see the fear in her eyes. Not one of her classmates stood beside her. They had removed themselves as if to prove that they were innocent. Sister turned to face them. 'What sinful children you are, believing lies put about by this girl or her father. What would he know about anything when he has a daughter who behaves as she does! Home, all of you, as fast as you can. I will decide what to do with you tomorrow. Surely it was a rabble like you that watched Jesus carry his cross!'

They scurried away in all directions closely followed by the now silent Bernadette. Turning towards the three of us Sister Gabriel smiled before asking the caretaker if he would be good enough to walk with us to our respective houses and this he kindly did.
We reached my house first, 'I will watch you in Vera' he said before continuing on the longer walk with my two friends.

The next day the headmistress was as good as her word and no more was said about the whereabouts of my friend's father. Looking back I can see that the two girls were protected for years by their mother's story. They could imagine their father miles away, trying to do the right thing for them. Just as they had been enthralled when he returned from the war with his stories of fighting and 'England winning!' their mother did have a story to tell; a story that was untrue but fashioned out of her love and her need to protect them both from the unavoidable repercussions of the truth.

The true story that the mother chose not to tell was full of pain but the contrived story saved her children from heartache for years until they could at least cope more ably with the truth.

Years later I met Barbara whilst shopping in Manchester. It was good to meet up again and to exchange news. Neither of us mentioned her father. I think that she must have realised that by then, like her, I had been told the true story and knew that he would spend a large part of his life locked up, being guilty of a despicable crime, but whenever I find myself as I often do in shops and market places surrounded by rolls of fabric and pieces of cloth if I get even a glimpse of green and pink gingham, I am reminded of the 'Milly Molly Mandy' dress, of Barbara, her sister, her mum and that spotlessly clean draining board. I have wonderful memories of my visits to that house, where I witnessed at first hand the demonstrative love the mother showed to her children. I saw the new baby when he came and was privileged to be part of their family life. With the help of the Sisters and people like my mother they did not go short of the basic necessities of life. My mother never mentioned my visits to them. It was as though the matter was a taboo subject, but I saw evidence of her kindness when ever Sister Gabriel and I emptied the contents of the basket.

One particular memory springs to mind, a story in itself. A much prized tin of peaches had been sitting on a shelf in our larder for months. My mother wrote on the outside of the tin the letters S.O...Special Occasion. It was to be saved. Imagine my surprise when one Saturday morning that same tin of peaches, complete with its initials, came out of Sister's basket. 'Not a word' Sister whispered and my lips were sealed!

Stories give people the chance to imagine and sometimes to link into memories woven carefully together. These images stay with us for a lifetime. I will never forget that part of my life, the way I felt at that time, it was all part of a story, the story of a small family, a nun and a young girl who carried a basket. Simple really, but never the less a story in itself.

Some stories become legends handed down from one generation to the next. One of my favourites is about an old American Indian chief who became concerned that some of the young braves in his tribe did not appear to be taking sufficient notice of advice that they were given by their elders.

These older Indians came to him. 'They speak too much of their own deeds' said one man.
'They speak before they have listened well to what we say' moaned another.

The chief observed the actions of these younger warriors. He knew how they felt inside their hearts. He looked also at the older men who had stood beside him in many battles. He saw inside their hearts too; but in all their hearts he felt that there was frustration and sometimes anger but no malice. How could he bring them together so that there would be a place for excitement as well as wisdom around the camp fire, which should be a place of great learning.

One day sitting beside the great river he watched as the water washed over the pebbles on the river's bed. Much to the consternation of the elders sitting a short distance from him he waded into the water and picked up a pebble with both hands and brought it to the bank.
Then he motioned to one of the men to carry it to his wig-wam.
Later that day he called them all together, the young bucks who spoke of nothing but fighting and the older men who had such great wisdom to share. 'Before each man speaks he must hold the stone in both hands' he told them. 'The stone must be passed between you and shall be known as 'the speaking stone'.' All of them understood his logic and marvelled at his wisdom.

Sometimes during my work I am asked to see children who have found difficulty explaining how they feel. So often this can arise when the child feels so unimportant that they listen but do not necessarily contribute to the conversation. This lack of confidence needs to be addressed. The introduction of a speaking stone accompanied by the story often helps them to speak more freely, as to hold the stone is to feel not only honoured but special. The stone is powerful too as only the person holding it can speak at that time.

Quakers believe that during their meetings members should speak only when they feel God's spirit move them. As a consequence, yet again, wisdom is shared first by listening, reflecting and ***only then*** making a comment of our own....how very wise.

Every single human being you know has a story to tell. Simply living from one day to the next is a story in itself and every story has a value.
Not just to the narrator, but to everyone who listens, whoever they might be.

Tonight before you get into bed, look into your mirror. Smile at the reflection there and remind yourself in a positive way that YOU are a storyteller. Better still, why wait until tonight, go to the mirror now and see the storyteller, who is YOU!

Time and tide waits for no man

Imagine a clock

Imagine a clock. A clock that tells us that the time is 12 o'clock, 12 o'clock noon or 12 midnight. It is not the hour that we should think about but the position of the hands both together joined on the figure 12.

Imagine that you are standing in life at 12 o'clock precisely. That you are standing just like the hands of the clock pointing from the centre to the number 12. You are upright. Standing in the present. If you turn the clock back to 11.45 you will be firmly in the past, 15 whole minutes into the past. If you turn the clock to 12.15 you will be firmly in the future. To take this example further try now to imagine that as you stand at 12 o'clock you are standing in a very worthwhile place, a good place to be, the present. All we can really be sure of is the present, the exact moment in which we stand. Looking back in our life transports us into the past and yet there is nothing there that can be changed. Nothing whatsoever can be changed even in the smallest way because it has already happened and therefore is unalterable.

All those words and actions which we know we have said and done we cannot take back, nor can we pretend that they have never ever happened. We cannot erase them or change them in any way. They have already been stated, uttered, proclaimed and heard by others. Yet not everything in the past is negative, much is positive and that is why our golden days, those days which contain the happy memories, can be stored and used to help us through.

Usually when we are tired and thoughtful, feeling

low or anxious, recalling the past rarely conjures up positive pictures, instead we usually remember everything we did wrong. If however we briefly consider what we perceive to be our mistakes and make a decision to try not to repeat them in the future, then our awareness is heightened and our personal growth progresses and what is more we will give ourselves more peace of mind. It is at this juncture that we can make a resolution and as we stand on the clock face of life at 12 o'clock we can decide that in the future we will not say the words we have said in the past.

What will bring about change? We cannot be sure that when the future comes we will not make similar comments or actions. But we can be sure about the minute in which we stand.

A great many problems in life are caused by the fact that as human beings many of us worry about our past experiences. It is a myth to believe that if we think about these experiences and consider them deeply then we will in some way bring about some healing.

Many have had the experience of an unhappy childhood, spent with unhelpful or uncaring people, or merely parents whose level of ignorance was high and whose level of sensitivity was low, such people will have experienced a past where love has been very very scarce but thinking about that childhood is not going to change what has happened. Standing at 12 o'clock firmly in the present you can make a decision to bring about actual change in your own life. You could even decide how you will speak to someone else, how you will behave, what you will do, where you will go. You can make a decision to be more considerate, more courteous, more well mannered or you can make a decision to be irritable, abrasive and abrupt.

Standing at 12 o'clock you can make these decisions and put them into practice.

Imagine now the hands of the clock telling us that the time is 12.15. There are many people who worry about the future. They actively dwell on it. Once I saw a cartoon of a man in a bowler hat, hunched shoulders, rubbing his hands together, a mournful expression on his face. Underneath the caption read "I am eagerly awaiting my next disappointment." Imagine ruining the prospects of the future by always expecting the worse.

"What will I do if I don't get the job, what will I do if the house doesn't sell, what will I do if he says he doesn't love me?" Winston Churchill once said "too many ifs accumulate". Elsewhere in this book I mention the way in which when someone dies so many of our sentences start with the words if. If only I hadn't shouted at him, if only I'd been more considerate, if only I had let her have that new dress, if only, if only. Those ifs belong in the past, nothing can be changed.

The ifs we place in the future give us cause for a great deal of worry however, because if we spend our time worrying constantly about the past and the future, there is very little that can be achieved as we stand on the clock face of life at 12 o'clock.

This is the present. This is the time to make change. If you feel the need to be different then make it now. If you want to improve the quality of your life or the life of someone else then do it now. Wishful thinking as we sit in a comfortable chair on a winter's evening talking about how we are going to live our life in the spring is all very well but we may not be around when spring-time comes. We need to be doing something now. This is the present.

Nothing is worth more
than this day

Johann Wolfgang von Goethe (1749-1832)

It is interesting to listen to the conversations of others, for conversations show us many, many aspects of someone's personality. A great deal of my time now is spent training professionals. Usually when the training is under way I watch their faces change. They start to look anxious and then eventually some brave soul will say "why didn't I know about this years ago, I've made so many mistakes."

It would be so easy at that time for me or any other trainer to say "you should have known better" but it would be entirely pointless. What I do suggest is that nothing can be done about the past, it cannot be changed but we could start now bringing about change. Recently a police officer looked aghast when in the course of training he learned of the way in which the news of death affected people. "I could have done my job a great deal better" he said, "I should have done it better, I should have known. What I am learning here is common sense, why didn't I know it". On many occasions we miss the complex message wrapped in a simple action and on other occasions we seek to complicate that which would be better understood when simplified. Always I explain to people who reach this point that although nothing can be done about the past they can never, ever, with a free conscience and a good heart make those same mistakes again because this time they know the difference. Being aware and knowing the difference is what enhances our life.

12 o'clock and all's well.

12 o'clock and here I stand straight to the point, firmly in the middle of my own present.

Recently in the course of a workshop one of those present was talking to me about my work. He described some aspects of how he saw my behaviour and then he said you are just like a coiled string. Of course, following on from his other comments I immediately thought he had said a coiled spring. When realisation dawned we laughed together. In fact I went on laughing for quite some time for in my mind there came a picture. First of all, a box containing a tightly coiled spring which when opened boinged and boinged about, springing out of the box onto a surface and going along its way and then I thought of a coiled string. I imagined myself looking into the box and seeing this worn old piece of string carefully placed in a few circles inside the box. Not going boing and not capable of going anywhere. Now if I had wanted to take a negative approach I could have been offended but I wasn't. I saw the laughter and the kindness in his face and I knew that there was not even the smallest chance that he meant anything but humour and fun by his comment.

At a conference once I listened to a very pompous man speak for boring hour after boring hour on a platform. As the audience were given permission to go and seek the solace of the cup that cheers in the interval I overheard one smartly garbed businessman say to another "that man is a legend in his own lunchbox". I found the comment hilarious having listened to the pomposity of this boring speech for hours, and the thought of him cramped and crumpled inside a lunchbox gave me a feeling of warmth that seemed to come up from my toes.

Humour is often linked very closely with confidence or indeed lack of it. So many of our comedians have stood on the edge of a nervous breakdown and looked inside a trough of despond. It takes confidence or the illusion of confidence to share our humour with others. Humour like laughter embraces others, takes them in, enfolds them and gives them permission to smile. Have you ever walked along the street smiling at people. The last time I did it one woman said to another "do you know her," "no" said the second woman, "neither do I" said the first, "silly beggar." But it was worth it to watch their faces, so I went back down the street and said "hello ladies, lovely day isn't it, no you don't know me, God's in his heaven and all's well with the world". They scurried off, giggling and laughing, it was worth it, it gave them something to smile about although I suppose it could be counted as very eccentric behaviour on my part! — and when it happened it happened in the present — the 'now' standing at 12 o'clock.

A close friend was beside herself with grief at the death of her husband, she did not know how she would manage without him.
A practising Quaker for most of her life she sought comfort from God and the members of her meeting house.
Old enough to be my mother she had influenced my life considerably whilst my children were young.
Although I wanted to give her comfort I knew what healing she found in silence. I therefore wrote the following poem for her.
Since that time it has found its way to many people in different parts of the world; people of all creeds and religions, agnostics, atheists and others who simply want to help but are not sure what words to say...

When I know there are words that you never quite say

When still tears in your eyes never quite fade away

When to speak would be foolish no matter how kind

Then I'll take you and hold you in my heart and mind.

In my prayers you'll be wrapped whether willing or no

Let them help and protect you wherever you go

Loss

For centuries there was an inevitability about birth and death but now with the advent of the birth control pill for women and a promised equivalent for men soon to be marketed we begin to limit that inevitability, however, at the moment we as human beings are experiencing difficulty in taking charge of death. With all our cleverness we can ease pain, give dignity to the whole process of dying but we cannot stop it happening.

At any time in our life we may experience loss and yet as a people in this particular country of ours we do not cope with the experience well. If you doubt this ask yourself how you have treated a colleague returning to work after a death within his family. If you can say I know I did the right thing then perhaps some lessons could be learned from you, however, if there is even the slightest hesitation when you think of this perhaps you fall into the category of people who wish they knew what to say or what to do.

Someone we love has died. Someone who means a great deal to us can no longer laugh or cry, touch or caress, speak or call. Someone we love is dead and in their place is emptiness and pain. We want them here, returned to us, so that we can be free of all the sentences that start with the words if only.

When death comes it leaves behind so much. If only I hadn't nagged your father, says the houseproud mother. I'd give anything for the mud from his boots to be on the carpet now.

But yesterday, last week, last year, it was a chore and she believed that she would have forever to nag him for he was hers and they had their life together.

The husband, grieving for his wife now dead, wishes that he had shown her more appreciation on long tedious shopping expeditions, and that perhaps he had said I love you, more often.

And then there are those of us who lose children. Asking ourselves repeatedly, Why, why, why. Why me? Why did God do this to me?

For often in our grieving God bears the brunt of our emotional pain. So many things that go wrong in the world can be blamed on man, but when we speak of death we often see the prime mover to be God.

Now we are left grieving, marooned on an island surrounded by the sea of our own fear, anger, frustration, depression, but seldom joy. And what do we feel if the loved one has died after a terrible illness? Dare we admit our feelings of relief that the pain and the suffering is now over? No longer the wincing with pain, the hospital bed, the stay in the hospice, the constant hurrying and scurrying to give support, all now gone, but dare we say I am relieved? Difficult.

How do we comfort one another? What do we say to those who are bereaved? How do we show them that we care? In our culture we are often very good at sending flowers and cards and these of course, are so important to the grieving family. Often treasured and kept for years. In many cases never, ever thrown away. But is it enough? Are we giving merely sympathy? I sympathise with you in your sad loss. I understand exactly how you feel. I know what you are going through. And yet in my heart I want to call out to the person who says these words. No you don't. You don't know exactly how I feel, you don't know what I am going through because he wasn't yours, he was mine. My partner, my father, my brother. She was part of my family, my mother, my sister, my child, and you do not know exactly how I feel, and yet we go on saying the words.

What is sympathy? The dictionary definition of sympathy is state of sharing, or tendency to share emotion, sensation, condition, etc., of another person or thing. So when you sympathise with me do I presume that you are trying to share my emotion, the feelings that I have? I ask myself do you really understand?

Empathy is however, a different matter. The Greeks tell us that empathy is to stand in the shoes and look out of the eye sockets.

When I am grieving, perhaps I long for you to stand in my shoes and to share with me the feelings of pain, disquiet and utter loss. If you were to give me your empathy then you would in fact, be looking at the world as I see it. I would know then that you understand.

Often difficulties arise in families immediately after the funeral. There is so much to do with death certificates, funerals and flowers, and bills to pay. Usually within the family emerges the leader, not always the natural leader, but a relative who will, in fact, take over and do that which has to be done. Not for this person the hours spent crying and showing visible signs of grief, but only the doing, the energy channelled into every task.

The funeral over, the family look about them to see what should be done next. All too often, a caring daughter or daughter-in-law, will decide that it is time that mum cleared out dad's things. Oh, if I only had a £1 for every conversation I had ever had with relatives in which the dialogue is as follows:-

Have you anything of your mother's left? Any article of clothing, something soft to the touch, because your father needs it at the moment.

Often there is nothing left, a whole lifetime cleared away in an afternoon, as busy daughters, sometimes helped by sons, clear out the room. Knicknacks kept which will remind them of a dear mother who is gone, but in the main, clothing dispatched to hospices, Oxfam and charity shops on the high street. But what of the griever? What of the partner who now finds himself sleeping in the arid desert that was once double bed in their years together, filled with love and passion, now empty?

To whom can this man say I am afraid? Yes, he can say I miss your mother, I wish she were here, but to whom can he express his deep, deep feeling of loss?

When I am counselling grieving people I suggest to them that they take an article of clothing that has belonged to the dead person, for whom they have felt so much love. I talk to them about the way in which at night they will curl up in a warm bed, and hug the garment to them. Yes I know that they will cry and cry, but perhaps better they cry than they fight to preserve an image of coping, usually designed to help others to cope more ably.

The garment will be hugged and the next day when the bed is made, the duvet cover is thrown back, the garment, be it a nightdress or a summer frock, will fall to the floor, from whence it will be carefully retrieved and folded up and put at the side of the double bed where the warm familiar body has lain for so long.

Time passes, and eventually one morning the grieving partner places the nightdress under the pillow, and then much later still, it falls to the floor and is retrieved and folded carefully and put in the drawer. This is the time of goodbyes for the grieving partner, not the time foisted upon him by well-meaning relatives, he has said his goodbyes at his own speed.

A health visitor telephoned me recently. I was unavailable in the office and my secretary answered. It was a strange message on the pad, it said tell Vera there is a cap on the hallstand. I knew exactly what she meant. She had telephoned me some weeks before to explain that she had done exactly as she had learned on one of our courses, with a patient. The old lady regularly took her husband's cap to bed, since it was all that was left of his belongings.

I spoke to the health visitor afterwards. With joy in her voice she told me how she had arrived at the house and seen the cap on the hallstand. Aye, said the woman, and it will stay there. It is the bit of him that will always be here. The treasured cap had made that long perilous journey from the bed to the hallstand. The worst part of the grieving had been endured. A small part of the ordeal already over.

Music plays a great part when we grieve. So many people have our song, or was it the song your mother sang so long ago whenever she was washing up? Or was it the lullaby your child so loved to listen to, when you put her to bed, and now her little bed is empty? Music may catch us unawares, and years afterwards, we find ourselves weeping copiously for something that was passed and is no longer tangible.

But if after the death we take a tape of the music we shared and go into a warm room and sit comfortably in a chair, all the better if we have a cat or a dog to stroke, a pot of tea, the fire on, we play the music, we weep. We play it again, we weep, we weep naturally, we weep in memory, but we have decided to do this for ourselves, we have put ourselves in charge of our own emotions, and never again will that song catch us unawares in quite the same way.

We have named it and claimed it, and though we may never throw it away, it is ours, the memory remains.

Help from the Professionals

[A few years ago the Nursing Times published an article that I had written especially for nurses. I felt that some nurses needed insight and help to give them confidence to cope more ably with grieving relatives. Part of that article is reprinted here.]

Today a woman stands in your ward, she gave her husband of forty years into your care - you, the nurse, the professional with training and expertise but most of all with answers.

When we take members of our families to hospital, we rarely take them there to die, for hospitals are filled with staff, most of whom wear uniforms. They are places of hope and enlightenment , not arenas of death. We believe the uniforms have a certain magic. We expect so much. This woman in her brown, somewhat shabby coat and lace up shoes gave you, the nurse, charge of her man. She trusted you and the doctors to do the best for him, your best. At home, she gave of her best with her spotless kitchen and his whiter than white shirts.

Now he is dead. Where are your words? What will you say because each word and gesture matters. They matter so very much, for at this moment you are the most important living person in her life. Some few weeks later she will remember with terrible clarity, not only the words you said, but everything else. A picture will come into her mind so clear, so defined in detail, that even the colour of your eyes will be recorded.

You, in your professional working environment, are preserved forever in the mind of another person. Some people say with great confidence that this is not so - 'I can't remember detail' - and then during a life crisis, or more often when they themselves go to hospital, they admit remembering.

You are busy. Time is short. The work in the ward never seems to stop. Things are not right for you at home. A relationship is going through a bad patch. You cope well with the routine - it helps to take your mind off what is troubling you but now, facing this relative, there is no routine to protect you. Guidelines, maybe, but no protection from that look of disbelief on her face. It is as though for a brief capsule of time, everything stops. How I respect and admire the nurse who gives of self in such a situation. Perhaps you work with her, or, better still, perhaps you are she.

She walks towards the relatives with kindness and warmth in her face. She takes them from the busy main ward to a side-room. She is already giving the message before she actually speaks. This break in pattern and procedure speaks volumes - and then with relatives seated, she explains - yes, she explains - that death has come; that despite the efforts of this capable team, death has outmatched them all.

She makes sure that the relatives are aware that she cares; that at that precise moment they are the most important people in her life. She seems to feel the pain with them. They, in turn, sense and know this. The comfort of emotional healing is immediately begun. How perceptive of the nurse who, at this point, decides to give the relatives a 'gift'. Perhaps she says 'Your Father was a lovely man, always wanting to help, and on his good days he'd get up and take tea to the others. We loved having him.'

Inappropriate comment? Oh no! For the relatives during their conversation in the future will say things such as: 'Sister said dad was really good in the ward. You know, I think they were sorry when he died'. What a gift given by a nurse with empathy. Empathy: To stand in the shoes and look out through the eye sockets.' Nurses have the opportunity to do just this so often. Empathy is not about empty sentimentality but about practical understanding. Just briefly, stand in their shoes. It takes but a moment.

Perhaps the most impersonal messages are given by telephone, until that special day an ordinary instrument of communication, usually made of plastic or metal. But today it is different, because through the wires, across town and country, comes a message that we do not want to hear and yet it comes.

Have you ever thought what an intrusion into privacy the telephone is? It rings when we least welcome or expect it. We may be in the bathroom, cooking a meal, having a quarrel, locking the front door, hanging out the washing, returning from work, key in the lock - and then - the telephone rings. We may like to comfort outselves by believing that trained staff give messages with kindness and care.

It is hoped this is so, but this was not one man's experience. He had taken his wife into hospital for two days for tests. He left her there in capable hands.

"I was just cooking some chips," he said, "when the telephone rang." A voice said:

"This is the hospital here - your wife has died."

No one in the ward admitted to giving the message - how could they? For weeks he never answered the telephone.

"I suppose I was afraid of it," he told me. "How silly at my age - I must be going mad." Silly, if we are assaulted emotionally, by whatever means, we take time to heal.

Sometimes people say: 'This can't happen at our hospital', but please, think about the people that you have worked with over the years. Perhaps one of them could be the sort of person who would behave in such a way. So easy to believe that if our own professional standards are high, so are those of other nurses. But is this always so?

A sister once told me how she had felt when a whole family, mother and two daughters, became hysterical as she told them of their father's death. They had walked into her ward and as she came toward them, had said:

"He's dead, isn't he? He's dead. Why didn't you do more?"

The three of them began to weep and the two daughters struck out at anything with reach, much to the consternation of patients and staff in the ward.

"What could I have done?" asked the sister.

She could have done very little. The family came with intent. They needed to blame someone, probably anyone, possibly because of their own desperate deep, emotional need, because they wanted time back to make amends.

Where possible, messages of death should be given in private to people already seated. Relatives should be given comfort, and yes, a cup of tea does help. Not only for its fluid contents, but because it gives the person something to hang on to. How we hug beakers and mugs when we are distressed. We almost caress them. We are quieted in spirit when our hands are thus occupied. People wring their hands when they are grief stricken. When we give comfort, the hands often become the least vulnerable part of the body. A man, a big man, told me how a staff nurse held his hands when his wife died.

"I didn't want her to take them away," he said.

Faith has an important part to play in the time of death and grieving. Those who believe in an after-life, a God of goodness or reincarnation, often find comfort in such beliefs. For God, the maker, can be given responsibility. He has a part to play. For those who see death as a doorway into a lighter life, quiet understanding of what they believe to be happening brings about easier, quicker acceptance.

A friend, who is a hospice nurse, spoke to me of a child whose mother requested that she, the staff nurse, explain to the son aged eight, that his daddy was dying. How well she did it; with such empathy.

"You know that your daddy is very ill?"

"Yes," said the boy. "I know he won't ride his bike anymore."

"Well," said the nurse, "your daddy is dying and he needs you."

At this the mother began to cry. The small boy put his arm around her and wiped her tears away with a tissue.

An eight-year-old boy? I think not. Perhaps a wise man hiding in a boy's physical frame. The nurse held their hands and comforted both of them. It was only as she recounted this experience that she remembered she had been eight years old when told that her own father had been killed in an accident. Nurses all over the country, indeed the world, give messages of death daily in busy wards, in peaceful hospices. They help relatives to cope. They do it to the best of their ability, but those who do it with empathy leave a lasting impression that will help towards the emotional healing that we as human beings so much need.

The final goodbye is important. Relatives need time to grieve. They find peace in various ways, like the woman who placed on the coffin of her husband a piece of wood carving he had done with immense pride and satisfaction.

"So that he'll know how much I shared his achievement," she said.

It was a March day, cold, with a biting wind. The petals of the early daffodils moved against the grained wood of the coffin. Family flowers for a dad mourned, but beside the floral tributes a little metal lorry, four inches long, given by a daughter to her lorry-driving father. 'So that he would always have his wheels.'

But where did this dying begin? With a doctor or nurse who said with feeling and understanding, but most of all, with empathy, 'I'm afraid your father hasn't long to live.' Watch the signs; think of the relatives or patient and put yourself in their shoes - albeit temporarily. In this way you will cope much more ably, and remember how very privileged you are to be involved in this most sensitive area of another person's life.

Acceptance

The other day on arriving in my office I was excited by the sight of a large package on my desk, it looked like a picture. I felt it, trying to guess what it was. Sure enough, it was a picture. On opening it I found it was a wonderful picture, the work of one of my clients. A restful picture in which to escape - the artist having captured the very heart of the place, green fields and little houses topped with a sort of sky that makes you want to book a holiday, flying of course, into that very sky.

The picture brought back memories of this particular client, a man who on coming to me the first time tried hard to act a part. It was all too much for him and after half an hour he dissolved into tears.

His emotional bank had experienced an overwhelming withdrawal; one of his colleagues shot dead, another wounded. Oh the futility of it all. After weeks of struggling he found he could cope no longer, the burden of his feelings and responses too difficult for him to carry. He sought my help with his load.

During the second session, on learning that he was an artist, I asked him to bring his portfolio. He willingly did so. Since the tragedy his paintings had changed considerably, most of the landscapes becoming brown grey or black, yet when we discussed the days on which the images had been recorded on canvass he remembered quite clearly that the weather had been very good.

Because he felt so empty, because he was suffering very deeply from what we call survivor guilt, he had become totally negative. After all, why should he live when another colleague was dead? Why should he see the sun and feel the warmth of it on his face? Why should he appreciate the fathomless sky or note the azure of its hue? It was no longer his entitlement.

Although at first he could not identify these feelings, through the counselling he began to understand. Together we made that special journey until he could feel more confident about himself, to grasp in his mind and heart that he needed to go on living, that this was his right. He needed to acknowledge life and his own positive gifts.

Over the weeks of our meetings, his art changed. He was lucky. So many people lose their artistic talent on becoming distressed. Because his drive and talent were so strong it was not easy for this to be cancelled out. It was not even temporarily destroyed, his art simply took another form. It became a way for him to express clearly his negative responses to his life, his work and to himself but most of all to his feelings of inadequacy. On that night, he, like so many of his colleagues, had been unable to save a life!!

This gift to me, his picture, the picture of the now, of the here, of life itself, is well balanced. It is a true record of what his eyes saw, not what his mind needed to view. It hangs in my office to remind me that it is possible to convert the negative response into a more healthy positive view of life.

Sometimes, when faced with death, we need another person to say that we have a right to go on living, that perhaps the belief that somewhere there is a book with dates, times and names and a God who makes the decision, can be helpful. This man came to the realisation that on the night of the tragedy it was not his time to go; only his time to feel inadequate and helpless in the face of something greater than himself.

He needed to be positive.

How do you like to go up in a swing,

Up in the air so blue

Oh, I do think it the pleasantest thing

Ever a child can do.

Robert Louis Stevenson

The Child's Eye View

The top of the mantelpiece glistened in the sunlight and although the day was warm a fire burned in the grate. The door at the side of the fire had a bright large shiny knob and a lady bowed at my feet. She wore a strange bracelet full of spiky little heads and I can remember a yellow soft glow about my body. Touching the yellow glow I felt good and whole.

This is my first memory, the first picture that my mind recorded that could be easily retrieved. After many questions and answers I discovered that I was describing a fitting I had had for a new yellow muslin dress. At that time I was two and a half years old. Of course the lady's spiky bracelet was the pad of pins attached with a piece of elastic around her wrist and of course she was not bowing to me but bending her head as she pinned together the pieces of my dress whilst I stood high up on what seemed like the top of the mountain, the mountain being her kitchen table.

My memories are vivid and clear, being full of colour whether bright or at other times dark colours full of foreboding. These are the pictures of my past.

Try sitting quietly in your favourite chair, let a piece of music play in the background, sitting there you can start the journey. Travel back and discover for yourself where your life of memories began. If you find that the first recall you can summon is at the age of 10 or 12 or later then sit and sit and trawl again for there will be some memories there, good, bad, indifferent. It is only when you can recall those memories of your own that you can begin to understand how children really feel and react to life. Of course this is a different age, a different generation, a whole new world now but still a child's reactions are basic to that child and the only way to understand the child is to understand the child that was once yourself.

Imagine a little boy returning from school. The childminder has collected him but in order to reach her house they have to pass his own. Strange happenings at my house he thinks. A sign in the garden. A sign just like the one in the garden of the house on the corner, a sign that says 'For Sale'. Where are we going he asks himself. The childminder looks frustrated and goes pink when he asks her what it all means.

"Your Dad will explain" she says "when he comes to collect you." The waiting for this small boy is endless, from 3.30 to 7.00pm he must wonder what is happening in his life. No one loved or confided in him enough to involve him in this situation. His parents had made the decision to move, never thinking of the anguish he would feel at finding a 'For Sale' notice outside his house, the house in which he has his bedroom in which he keeps his precious toys and his little treasures.

No, I am not for one moment suggesting that you ask tiny children their opinions in matters of great importance for of course a small child may not understand. However, to warn him of what is happening puts him confidently in the picture. A man once said to me "we only told the twins two days before we moved because we didn't want to worry them." The twins as he collectively called them had known for months simply by following the clues. No 'For sale' sign in their garden but the constant tidying up and boxing away of their toys, to say nothing of the contents of the garage told them its own story. Why oh why do so many adults presume that children simply do not understand what is happening in their lives.

Even a small child is capable of understanding and in the absence of any explanation will, more often than not, put in place guessed information of their own. Often this information is totally incorrect. With "fobbing off" comments from the adults in their life they struggle to discover what is actually happening. Just like the boy who said after his father and mother had parted "well, my mum and dad didn't speak together for a long time". "Not so" yelled his mother, "he couldn't have known" she said, turning to me. "Well" said her young son "you put his pyjamas in the big bed every morning and made the little bed up to look tidy before I got up every morning." Incredulously his mother stared in silence. How did he know? At seven she didn't realise he had made it his business to know what was going on in his own house. He was tired of the sound of raised voices as he went to sleep. The banging in the night, the slamming of doors and the perceived front of hypocrisy in the morning.

Children who are given ongoing information about happenings in their lives cope much better. It is for instance always difficult to know whether to tell a child that one of their parents is dying. If the death seems to be some way off then small words of preparation need to form themselves so that the child learns lessons about the fact that not everything or anything lives forever. With a lot of love this awful information can be passed on to the child, assimilated and later acted upon.

If you gather together a group of six and seven year olds, win their confidence and talk to them intimately about the happening in their lives, they will give you information that will increase the depth of your wisdom to such a degree that you will wonder how you had existed in life without it. The small boy who says "when my mother says we'll see, I know its never going to happen, when my daddy says one day, that's a non event as well." Children are easily fobbed off but they are often given a double or dual morality. Take for instance the situation in which we often place them without realising, that we are placing upon them two different standards of behaviour.

Take an ordinary family; mum and dad, caring, working hard, wanting their children to grow up with honesty and integrity. There are rules of the house and home, there are rules regarding behaviour and the way in which they speak to one another but one rule prevails, that of truth, so mother says "we will not have any lies or untruths here" and children live by that code. In all too short time those same children realize that his code does not exist for their parents, it exists only for them and as one boy put it "it's because you have only have to do those things when you are little and not when your grown up." I am referring of course to our natural hypocrisy when dealing with other people. Tea time for this family sitting around the table, conversation as follows:-

Mother: "You will never guess what happened at the Carter's today. A man came and took away quite a lot of furniture, looked like the bailiffs to me but then of course we know how much money she owes everybody."

Father grunts "well things have been difficult for them."

Mother: "That's no excuse, she owes everybody in the street and I'll bet she owes more money on her clubs than anyone else."

The children, ears like windmills, take in this information and inwardly digest — so the Carters up the road owe money. Judging from the conversation around the tea table the Carters are not liked by mum and dad. In fact, as the conversation continues it becomes more than evident that they are distinctly disliked.

Now children can cope with this because they have friends whom they dislike for no apparent reason. They in their kindness give the same licence to their adult counterparts but then how do they cope when the scene continues with a knock at the door, the door opening and Mr. Carter on the doorstep saying "I wonder if I can come in and have a word." False smiles all round, oh come in, come in. The children sit at the tea table quite baffled, here is Mr. Carter who father and mother have spent the last half hour criticising and he is in their house and now he is being offered a cup of tea, offered a cup of tea by two people whom these children respect, who they know dislike Mr. Carter intensely. The children in the family are faced with a dual morality, they have nowhere to go with it but they learn from it and they become aware that it is quite all right to be nice to someone's face and critical to them behind their back. The parents have forgotten the maxim which should prevail which says "if you can say nothing good, say nothing at all."

When I was a child this situation regarding parents and adults was brought home to me in rather a curious way and I can only hope that in later years the lady and gentleman involved forgave me for my tremendous *faux pas.*

I had heard my mother and father talking together about a woman who was a neighbour of ours further up the street. I heard them refer to a friend of hers whose name was Bernard as her fancy man who was never away. Later that day when walking up the street I saw Bernard in the garden of the lady neighbour. He was helping her to weed her herbaceous border. I climbed on to the garden gate and looked over at them both. They smiled and waved. I liked Bernard, I thought he had very kind eyes. I looked at him for a long time trying to decide what part of him was fancy. His shoes were just plain brown and his long sleeved shirt which he had rolled up to the elbows was just like those that my father wore. His trousers weren't particularly fancy either but then perhaps my father and mother were referring to his braces because they were a little fancy but not enough I thought for him to be called "a fancy man."

Mrs. Leeming went into the house and brought out two large glasses of lemonade and a smaller glass for me. "Come in Vera" she said, "don't stand on the outside of the gate, come in and sit down on the grass and have a drink with us." It was in those days when such invitations could be trusted, where there was no marauding evil to be perceived. I drank my lemonade and continued to survey Bernard until at last he asked me if there was anything the matter. I said "No." "What are you thinking?" he asked. "I am trying to decide how fancy you are." Mrs. Leeming looked at me "what do you mean Vera, fancy?" "Well" I said "my mum and dad said Bernard is your fancy man and I am trying to think which part of him is the most fancy." There was a deathly silence. Their two pint glasses were placed upon the tray. They smiled sad little smiles at me and I realised that in some awful way I had hurt them but I had no idea why. I began to feel uneasy so I said my goodbyes and left the garden which suddenly didn't seem sunny and warm anymore. Later that night when I was ready for bed I said to my father and mother "I saw Bernard today with Mrs. Leeming." "Oh yes" said my father. "I told him you said he was a fancy man and that I was trying to see what you meant but only his braces were really fancy." Another deathly silence and then my father looked at me and said nothing and my mother told me I was the most stupid girl she had ever met in her entire life.

So the stupid eight year old went to bed with no notion as to what she had done or not done, other than the knowledge that in some way without her knowing she had caused sadness in the faces of two adults and anger and frustration in the faces of another two adults. There were no explanations and it was many years before I realised just what I had done. Please include your children. You are privileged that a child comes into your life and that you are allowed to care for that child, to give the child love and have love in return but the child needs information as much as love, information that will help him or her to feel secure. Scant information, incorrect information, gossipy information gives the wrong messages and innocent people including the child suffer as a result. So the next time you find that you are about to say of your child "he doesn't understand," ask yourself if it's you that doesn't understand how much he could understand. Now there's a daunting thought!

Imagine the scene. I will try to paint a picture in words for you. Recently while visiting friends in Malta an invitation was extended to share a typical Maltese Sunday. No Yorkshire pudding or Sunday roast but something very different yet enduringly comforting. The Maltese usually go to church on a Sunday as a family, even teenagers are expected to accompany their parents. After church the families meet together talking animatedly, gesticulating, laughing together. Much more touching here in this Mediterranean island, with inhibitions much less obvious. Some families then return to their homes but for the majority a meal out is the order of the day. Flocking to their favourite restaurants they eat together. Families joined by boyfriends, girlfriends and others.

Small children also have their place within the family and there's always a helping hand for the little ones. For in Malta children are valued though the moral code is strictly adhered to, respect for parents and an abundance of love is ever present. After the meal, a walk. All the family walking, tiny tots on sturdy plastic bikes, grandparents, parents, and children, all together for Sunday. A small boy holds his mother's hand as he walks along on a sea front pulling a car behind him on a string, a little girl with glasses pulls at her mummy's hand and asks about her shadow and why it is getting longer and longer. Parents here converse with children ensuring that they have a special place in the heart of the family. There is much talking and interest in the world of the child. Was this how we once were a decade ago, two, three decades past? Did we respect our children in that way then?

What has happened to so many people, and why has there been such a change in our society? Is it because we live more in the fast lane then ever before?

The little boy who still has time to pull a car behind him on a string will give comfort to many, his very action showing that there is time in life for the simpler things.

In Malta the drivers constantly honk their horns at one another, they wave and shout and in a traffic jam a cacophony of sound can be heard as driver after driver press their horns repeatedly. This is no road rage though, it is accepted here that this is how people express themselves. There is nothing vicious about their actions. They show their feelings of joy and friendliness whilst we within our culture often suppress ours. It is no accident that in Malta the cases of mental illness are less per head of the population than here and that certain other illnesses are not as prevalent. Letting off steam can in itself be comforting, the driver honking his horn in a non aggressive manner in Malta still has time to spend with his child and in the meantime he has given vent to his pent up feelings in company with his fellow countrymen.

Round and Round

'Life and death are one, even as the river and the sea are one.
For what is to die but to stand naked in the wind and to melt into the sun.'

Kahlil Gibran

Round and round and round.
Still no hint of blue. No blue at all.
Tom, where are you?
How long have I been sitting here, watching for a glimpse of blue material behind the glass porthole of the washing machine? Perhaps today I will see one of your grey socks. It will be an odd sock, one of a pair and when I take the washing out I will wonder for at least the hundredth time why it is singly tangled in amongst the other clothes.
I kid myself, a joke a laugh on me.
It won't be there today because you are gone.

You told me that you loved the colour blue.
My favourite you said and why not, sky and sea are blue.

'Yes, 'it's my favourite' you repeated and we stood and laughed together.

There are no boxer shorts.
Blue, white, grey, patterned, plain all gone, nothing left of you...
Your side of the big oak wardrobe is full of emptiness, hangers that jostle each other when I open the door. How could I have let it happen?
Karen was sure it was the right thing to do. She'd read the book!
Tom, imagine our lovely Karen had bought a book to tell her how to grieve for her dad. Oh where did we go wrong?
'It's what we need to do' she said 'it will be best for mum.' It didn't take very long at all for them to erase you, to cancel you out. Her brother's wives Felicity and Miriam; they all knew what to do.
Shirts and jackets to the thrift shop.
Overcoats to the homeless shelter together with your shoes.
They even threw away the knobbly woolly sweater that you'd had for years. Or at least they think they did.
I should have said something my love.
If it were now I could. Is it really eight weeks since we were saying our last goodbyes at the crematorium. They only gave me two days, Tom, and then everything changed. Our sons were no help, they simply did what they were told.
I heard Miriam saying that they had to watch out for the signs that I was making a 'shrine' to you. A

shrine? There isn't enough of your things left in this house to fill a box, let alone a shrine.
Tom, I want to see your blue shirt, your socks, I want you back here with me just as we were.
Where are you?
Karen was kind. She wanted me to go and live with her and the children. I was tempted at first. Surrounded by the little ones I would feel loved but it meant leaving our home, everything that reminds me of you.
Because I missed you so much, or was it because I felt afraid that I agreed to go and stay just with her but I was glad to get home.
Guess you know that already.
It was strange coming back to this old house. It felt empty and cold although the heating was turned up. It was the sort of cold that gets inside your bones.
After Karen dropped me off I simply sat and cried. I didn't notice that it was dark. It felt so strange going around switching on the lamps. Then, Tom, something strange happened. I began to feel afraid just like I'd felt when I was a little girl.
So I decided to light up every room in the house and when I finally went to bed I left the bedside lamp alight. Your lamp Tom...at your side of the bed.
The bed is so big now and empty. It feels enormous. I know that it is just the same as always. Do you remember the day when we bought it?
Too high you said and I said, 'I like high'. We both laughed as we lay on top of the mattress together holding hands in the middle of the shop.

When they packed your clothes I saw the 'gaffer' tape.
Felicity had bought it specially. 'We all need to help' she smiled.
I didn't want to smile Tom. I wanted to yell and say 'Your father-in-law has rolls of that tape in his garage. He uses it for everything. You only needed to ask. You didn't have to waste your money'.
Instead, I didn't speak; can you imagine, I just stayed silent. Without you beside me I felt afraid to say anything. It's different now. Just a bit. That's why I'm sitting here holding your knobbly sweater. I sneaked out and took it from a box in the back of the car. Tom.... I felt like a naughty schoolgirl stealing something. They don't know!

You are still here with me somewhere, seeing me snuggling this old sweater everyday. I can't sleep without it. It smells of you Tom, my lovely man.
Well, they are all getting on with their lives now. It is as though their tears are over. Mine aren't, I still miss you.
Me, I sound so mean and begrudging. They do miss you. The words they said at the funeral were their own, what they really felt about their dad but they have moved on whilst I seem to be standing still!
At last I have managed to sort out all the direct debits at the bank. You always insisted that you did all of that. Well, I can do it now. Tom, I have to say I'm a bit angry at you about all of that. The bills, direct debits in fact all the bank stuff. You used to say I was not to trouble my head, that you being a man had that all in hand. Why didn't you

show me what to do just in case you went first...or did you think that as a man you were bound to live longer!
Looks like I will have to change the car. Get a smaller one. Our old four by four is alright but I can't reach to change the oil and water. The neighbours are so kind but I can't keep relying on them. They have their own lives and let's face it Sid next door is not getting any younger and young Jan and Phyl have busy lives.
You did so much. I loved the way you took care of me but I wish that I had taken more interest in that side of our affairs. Now there seems to be so much for me to learn. Was I always so helpless? It isn't simply that I miss you every moment of everyday but sometimes I'm angry because you are gone and I'm still here, trying to cope. You said you would never leave me.
Do you remember Peggy? She sent me a lovely sympathy card. I haven't seen her for years. She came to see me. At first she listened. I needed that and then she said that she knew exactly how I felt. It's a lie Tom.
How could she know? She married that awful Fred that lived near the park. Tom, she kept repeating the words 'I know exactly how you feel.'
All I wanted was for her to go so in the end I asked her to leave.
It was then I felt this word coming up inside my throat Tom, I wanted to swear at her and push her out of our house. It was awful. I finally said 'Peggy, I'm sorry Fred died but you don't know exactly how

I feel. You only know how you felt when it happened to you'.
Do you know what she said Tom, she said that it was the same, we had both lost our husbands and if I wanted people to sympathize I needed to treat them better? Needless to say I haven't heard from her since. You are nothing like her husband.........!
That night I was sure that I wouldn't sleep but I did. I slept better than I'd slept for days so perhaps it wasn't all bad.

The doctor gave me some tablets. He said they would help. I didn't take them, it would take more than a pill to bring you back.
You said that when you retired we would do all those things that we never got time to do, with the family and work and everything.
That first year without your work, we did nothing. The second year was just the same and here we are five years on and now it is too late.
Well, dear heart, the washing programme has stopped.
Time to take everything out.
All my clothes.
None of yours.
Tom, do me a favour, send me a sign.
Just let me know that you are watching me from somewhere, heaven, that place whatever it is that we go onto after this life, even God seems to have deserted me!
Please, just a small sign.....Tom.....anything will do..........

Tom's wife came to see me on a few occasions. She did not need deep therapy, she simply wanted to talk about Tom and to have help in understanding what was happening to her since his death.
She loved the term life-coaching...no stigma she said. 'You are simply helping me to cope. Tom would approve.'
No, she did not tell her family that our meetings took place. 'It's just for me' she smiled.

Grieving takes many forms. There are numerous books that attempt to tell us how to grieve. However, just as we are unique individuals so the way in which we mourn our loved ones is equally personal. How easy it would be if we could say this will happen or that will happen. We do need time to mourn, time to wish that we had said all that needed to be said. We need time to forgive ourselves for continuing to live after the one we hold dear has died. Time to review the past before we can store it where it can be borne more comfortably.
Emotional pain is part of the grieving process. It is allowable, the weeping, the thoughts, the anger and frustration, we are human and these are natural reactions to death.
Reviewing the past may happen simply without us being aware that it is taking place. The memory cells function in various ways. No two people react in an identical way.

Where there is grief, there is often an absence of logic, at least for a while. Try not to expect too much of yourself.
For centuries human beings had no control over death or birth.
However with the progress in medical science it soon became apparent that birth could be controlled and life changed for millions of people, particularly women, who began to feel that they were in control of at least one aspect of their lives. Death however remains a mystery. Sitting one night with a very sick lady lying in a hospice, as I bent closer to her she whispered 'Vera, death is standing at the door, don't let him in until my son gets here.' The son in question was flying in from Australia. Death is totally beyond our control, coming at any time, sometimes totally without warning, but as so often happens the lady waiting for her son died in his arms.

Those with deep enduring faith often feel much more assured at the thought of death, believing that there is a place, a good place, to which we go after we die, namely heaven. Different religions, different beliefs, but all can be reassuring.
When we are close to someone who dies accidentally or suddenly we are affected in many different ways. A man whose workmate died in a building site accident described how afterwards he valued his own life more than ever. Things left undone needed to be finished, dreams and goals realised. He described a sense of urgency and went out to buy the new car that he had hesitated

about...only one life he said. This is often associated with survivor guilt when we ask ourselves why we were saved and the person who stood next to us only minutes before dies inexplicably.
One of the answers to the puzzle of death is to accept that we must seize the day, this day, this moment, it is the only time we can be sure about.
Tom's wife will recover eventually. Time does not necessarily heal us completely. What really happens is that we find as each week passes we can carry the burden of our grief a little more easily. The first year is the most difficult. Birthdays, anniversaries, Easter, Christmas, that first Christmas often the hardest of all but we have to go on with our lives. Keeping busy is important and learning to look after ourselves in a positive way. It is during this period that we need to become aware of the fact that as those around us get on with their everyday lives they can find us to be poor company. Sympathy does not last forever. The father who says constantly that he wishes that he had died with his wife places such guilt on those around him that one would wonder at his selfishness. Yes we do say those things at the outset but the man who comes to see me a year after his wife's death need not wonder why his children so dread his visits. 'What can we do?' his grown children ask. 'She was our mum and we miss her too. Doesn't he see that we are grieving but we have children, our own lives, we have to go on!'
Such conversations are commonplace.

At this time in your life surround yourself with as much light as you can, no point in sitting in the darkness. Try to eat little and often, you can easily feel overphased by the appearance of food. Monitor the programmes that you watch on the T.V. no use in becoming more maudlin as you view violence and bloodshed. Play the music that you like, it may have been a shared choice and as you listen you may shed a silent tear. Memories are not cancelled out by grief, try to recall all the happy times you spent together and should there be feelings of bitterness and frustration throw them away, such feelings and thoughts will achieve nothing now.

A few weeks after the death, friends often cease to visit as often as they did when it first happened. Sadly it is usually about this time that we can remember with a terrible clarity the person who is gone. Always try to keep a garment or something soft that has been close to your loved one, you will need to hold it again particularly at this time. Breath in the smell of love that remains in the garment; we all have our own scent. Attempt to look at family and friends from a different angle; ask yourself what is happening in their lives, do they have a need to talk, is it your time to listen?

Oh and by the way be assured that there is no shame whatsoever in talking to the dead person and No, you are not going out of your mind. You may have known them, loved them, talked to them for years, death is not a complete full stop in the story of our lives. Our loved ones have merely passed on.

Fred believed in 'nothing'. 'There is no God, no afterlife it is just a black hole'. His wife had died of cancer two months previously.
'It is just a black hole. She is gone!' he told me.
I waited, he was silent for a moment and then he said 'you are supposed to make me feel better, tell me there is a God and all that; just like *she* believed. Well, say something!' With that he burst into tears. And I was reminded of the quote 'The lady doth protest too much, but this time it was Fred, aged fifty. Fred, who later told me that he wanted her back so that he could apologise for the affairs that he had and suddenly the concept of the black hole was no comfort.
So we talked of other beliefs, mostly the belief that his wife as a devout Christian held dear. He knew the words, the quotations, he was word perfect. Many people have written that belief comes out of weakness and need, does it really matter? Fred needed comfort and eventually found that much needed peace sitting in the church that his wife had attended alone for years. 'I thought they were just a bunch of gossiping do-gooders' he told me 'but they really loved my Louise they made me so welcome'.

I like the quote of Billy Wilder who said, when asked about Faith and belief, 'I have no problem with the pilot but the ground crew give me cause for concern'.

Well the 'ground crew at Louise's church gave of their best!

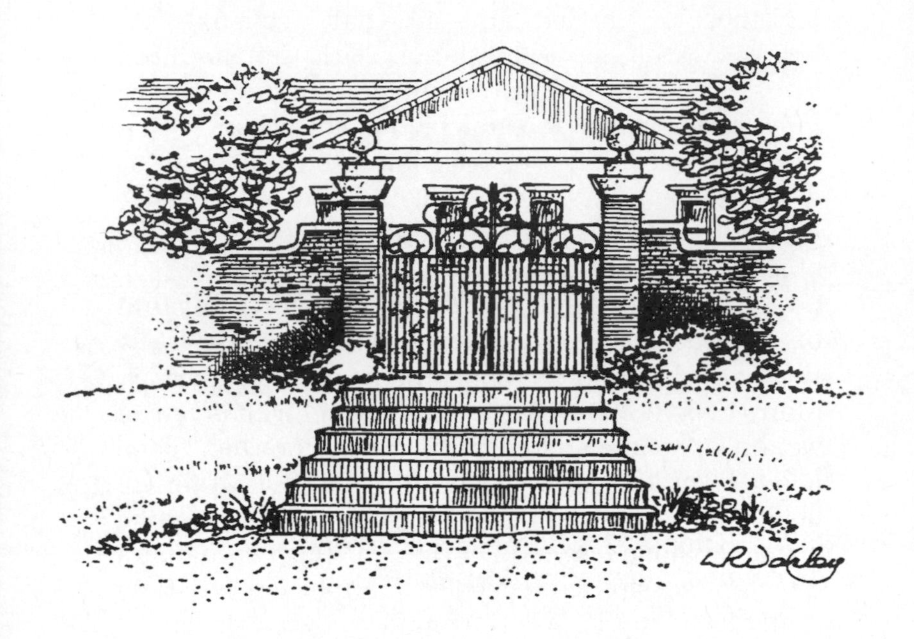

Scarborough Steps

If we are to accept the importance of the Emotional Bank then we need to also acknowledge the Power of Parenting. The nature v nurture argument should not be seen within controlled restrictions. Both have a part to play in the development of the human being. Why is it that certain people when faced with the most incredible hardship somehow, through it all, survive? Could it be that the love given to them as children helps them to face life's adversities and they seem to draw on their Emotional Bank which because of their upbringing shows a healthy credit.

The following glimpses are taken from life, we could perhaps call them Parents in Action.

The place is Scarborough, it is summer, I see a father with his son. The little one looks about three years of age, he is walking along the sea front laughing and giggling. Together, the two of them, now stand at the top of a huge flight of stone steps. Hand in hand, they take the steps one at a time each in step with the other, striding out together. The father, one leg poised, waits for the shorter leg of his son to catch up. Plod, down go their feet. The son looks up at his daddy. Many people on the steps today, making their way up or down towards the beach. But this couple taking the short journey together with happiness and obvious shared joy are to be remembered. In later years, the boy then grown to the man, will remember the love and patience of his father.

But here comes another family. Father again, but this time joined by mother and son. This small boy runs towards the steps and looks down the flight but his face shows signs of trepidation. The steps are steep, he is afraid. He puts out his hand to his father seeking reassurance, the little fingers moving, catching air, but father does not take his hand,

"Go on" he shouts "it's just a few steps, get on down."

He does not join his son but stands at the top of the flight waiting for the small boy to move. The little hand falls to his side, one small foot fleetingly touches the top of the first step, but the little fellow steps back, afraid. Father comes nearer, now obviously angry.

"Get on, don't be so soft."

The little boy looks to his mother, but she avoiding his eyes looks away. She does not see the small bottom lip quivering.

Suddenly the scene is changed. A large friendly hand grasps the small one, a woman passing has bravely intervened, sensing the dilemma of this little boy.

"Come on my sweetheart, help me down the steps" she says in a loud, warm friendly voice. The boy smiles as hand in hand these strangers, young and old, make their way companionably down the steps. Father shows surprise, stands hands on hips surveying the situation which has been taken from him. He at that precise moment having no power or control. Mother relieved briefly glances at father, worried and afraid, she looks away quickly. Father, a strange smile crossing his face, starts to descend and joins the stranger now at the foot of the steps.

She is talking to the little boy, their conversation is

animated. The little boy likes her face and her warm soft eyes. Father says

"They're all soft at this age but I'll make a man of him yet!" The little boy looks up at his daddy, there are no words said but it is as though his eyes speak out for him, but daddy, daddy, I'm only three, I don't want to be a man yet, I am only little and I want your love.

Children are like birds, they fly into our lives, nest for a while and then as quickly as they came they are gone, flying on to other places, other people, other words. Never once may we own our children, they are born as free spirits, their freedom, their right to freedom, is their own!

Parenthood — The Follies and the Love

The other day, walking along Deansgate in Manchester, I saw ahead of me a young mother looking distraught, by her side but standing quite separately, a small boy of about four years and his sister who was possibly all of six years old. As I drew near, the mother, nervously glancing this way and that, approached me.

"Where's the Magistrates Court?" she asked.

"It is nearby" I reassured her. "A few minutes walk away."

"Oh," she said and strode off in the direction I had indicated. The little boy seemed taken, however, by my pink lensed glasses and lingered a few precious seconds to look at them more closely. I winked at him and he tried manfully to wink back, but was obviously not totally sure of how to wink.

But his long legged mother had set off at a sprint, soon outpacing his little sister valiantly trying to keep up. The boy looked up at me.

"She's gone." he said.

"No," I said, "She's there, you'll catch up with her."

Oh the foolishness of grown adults who make inane

statements to wise young people! Even I should have seen that it was impossible.

How could he reach his mother? She'd crossed Deansgate at the traffic lights, looked once, bawled to her daughter and was gone. Before I could stop him he was away too, running, crying, stumbling, he fell, his small nose hitting the pavement. He howled, but it was not his mother who turned to his aid but his little sister.

Halfway across the busy road she sped back and as I helped him to his feet she, little mother, breathless with running, took his little face in her hands and said

''It's all right Ben, you're not really hurt, don't cry.''

''She's gone,'' he said into her face.

''It's all right. I know where she is.''

Before I could say another word, she took his hand and, waiting till the traffic lights had changed to green, she then guided him across Deansgate. A six year old girl, going on 40, a caring loving soul. I feared for them. Staying a few paces behind them, I followed them to the opposite corner. There, angry, their mother waited.

''Are you stupid or something?'' She took the boy's hand and prepared to smack him.

In a quiet voice I said

''No, he did his best, you walked so fast he could not have reached you. Why smack him for something he could not achieve?''

Her angry eyes blazed into mine and I waited for the rebuke.

''Aren't you lucky?'' I said as her mouth fell open. ''So lucky, your two children are so very beautiful, where does their beauty come from? You must cherish them so much.''

She looked at me as though I had lost my mind.

''Beauty?''

She shouted into my face.

''These two beautiful?''

''Oh yes,'' I said, ''can't you see it? Everyone else can.''

She turned and I began to walk away. I turned to see that she had stopped again and was staring after me.

For a few seconds I held her gaze and then she stalked off, holding in her hands the hands of each of her children.

"Beauty!"

I could hear her saying,

"Beauty!"

Children are merely birds that fly into the nest of our lives and then they fly out again. But if we are parents we are so lucky that they come at all, to bless us with their wisdom and their understanding and to give us a space in which to learn.

Nowadays there are some books that are written by very clever, erudite people on parenting, but often when our children are born we cannot find such a book, or perhaps we do not have the inclination to read it if we could. We set about this task, foolishly thinking that if there is enough love in our hearts we will be successful.

Often a voice in our head says, I will not make the mistakes my parents made, and often we manage to hold to that rule and we don't. But, alas, we often make a new set of mistakes all our own. We stamp them Copyright. Our mistakes are shiny and new, brilliant in the morning sun, mocking us, letting us know that perhaps, just like our parents, we didn't get it right all of the time.

But what of our children who wait for us to be big enough and confident enough to say to them In your opinion, what do you think we should do? A three year old has opinions and with the right guidance they can become worthwhile.

Some years ago an acquaitance visited our home. It has always been our custom whilst the children were with us to use the evening dinner table as a place to present problems, to tell jokes, to have fun. No silence at table for us I'm afraid!

My daughter was three at this time and whilst we were discussing a particular situation, I asked her what she thought of it. The visitor was appalled.

"What on earth are you asking her for?" she said. "She's too small to understand."

I smiled at her. "How do you know?" I asked.

"But she is."

"How do you know?"

Children need a chance, a chance to express themselves, but most of all a chance to learn about their own world. The little boy falling on his nose would not get a sense of self-worth from his mother, she is too busy growing up herself.

He may get some from his protective sister, but where will she get hers from? Who will hold her and tell her that she is beautiful? Who will enable her to have confidence? This mother with the long legs dashing on ahead, not caring whether the children can catch up with her or not? I hardly think so because, you see, perhaps this mother has no sense of her own worth either.

Do you value the child or children that live in your home? Are they considered? Are they asked what they feel and think? Do you ever sit your little boy or girl, just old enough to start school or playgroup, on your knee and ask him or her what they feel inside? How will they know about feelings unless they are identified?

One day out in the big world your child will have a need to walk tall, to look in the mirror and like at least some of what he sees. He cannot do this without your assistance. He needs to know that at the end of the day if the whole world is against him that you, his parents, care, that you love him despite everything.

We are wise to say to our children I will love you for ever, but I cannot always guarantee to like you, because in the course of your development, in the strength of your growing, you may well have experiences and behave in a way that I do not like. But that dislike of your actions will never, ever, spoil the love that I feel for you. So much security in a statement that helps a child to decide what loving and liking are really about.

I hope that somewhere in the world there is someone who can say to those two small children on Deansgate: I love you, whatever you do I will always love you. Perhaps their young distraught mother cannot do that. Maybe she doesn't know anyone in the world who loves her, warts and all. She may, therefore, have great problems passing on a positive philosophy and guidelines for living but so much may be learned from standing back and identifying with her words and actions.

The Hairdressers

The other day I went to the hairdressers, I was early for my appointment and this meant waiting for about 10 minutes. I occupied myself by looking out through the window at the busy main road.

The hairdressers is quite close to a set of traffic lights. The cars speed along and then grind to a halt when appropriate.

Across on the other side of the road I saw a young woman, tall and slim, striding along the road purposefully. I did not immediately notice that she was holding the hand of a very small child, but I glimpsed the child's feet barely touching the ground as she strode along. The mother was like an arrow aimed from a bow, going towards a target. The child however, seemed to have no target at all, she being merely equipped with a pair of little feet that hardly touched the ground. It was easy to see that the child's arm was pulled taut, actually as taut as it could go. The child's face too was strained, little brow frowning. Hard to tell if this child was a boy or a girl, it had been raining and she, if she was a she, was wearing one of those sexless toddler's raincoats.

Then, suddenly the woman obviously became angry, her strides lengthened. She shouted at the child. Because of the distance it was impossible to tell exactly what she was saying. As she spoke she jerked the child's hand cruelly, pulling the taut little arm even more. The little feet flew into the space immediately above the ground, and at that second the child would be aware that she was in mid-air.

But this was not a mother playfully swinging the child, making sure that the child was safe. This was a mother either too angry or too self-centred to notice what the child was really about. Her life was probably full of worry. At that moment she interested me, in fact they both interested me. I walked out of the hairdresser's to the edge of the pavement, the better to watch them until they were out of sight. I reckon that it took four or five of the child's tiny steps to measure one stride of her mother's lanky legs.

Mother had no eye contact with the child, barely a look passed between them, although the child beseechingly looked up the long arm to the shoulder, trying to make contact with the face. Mother's movements were about anger and a total lack of concern for this small human appendage attached to her right hand.

Afterwards, as the hairdresser dried my hair, I thought again of the mother. I wondered if anyone had ever explained to her what a child feels like. I remembered a small boy of four, whose name was Richard, he and I met several years ago. I could hear him across the years, responding to a question.

I had asked him to describe his little world. After much thought he said

"There is a lot of legs."

Richard knew a great deal about legs and shoes and skirts, he knew a great deal about his mother's legs, his father's legs and very little about his own. But when you are a toddler the world is full of legs.

Often children dislike being placed on high objects. Their feet dangling a thousand yards from the security of the floor. Sometimes we hear the father or mother having placed the child on a precarious perch saying that magic word jump, first proffering their outstretched hand. Well, I ask you, if you were much less than 2' tall placed on a 5' high wall or something similar, would you jump off into oblivion? Even though your father or mother said you should. Often the parent persists, jump they shout, jump, it will be all right.

Yes daddy, all right for you nearly 6' tall, feet firmly placed upon the ground whilst I sit here on my perch, my feet dangling in space, wondering whether I should trust you enough to jump.

The little girl with the lanky legged mother will also know a lot about legs. She will have a tired arm when she gets wherever they are going. She will be fractious and then 'they' will say she is short tempered and irritable. She may well fall asleep over her mid-day meal. Someone supposedly much wiser, will decide she should go to bed earlier, or take a nap now.

Who will advise her mother of this mis-use of parent power, I wonder?

Twinkle, twinkle little star
How I wonder what you are
Up above the world so high
Like a diamond in the sky

Traditional

A Bit Of Magic

Many people worry a great deal about the way in which children may react when told of the death of someone they love. Before we talk about how they may or may not react in such circumstances, we need to consider how we as adults respond when given such news, how we as individuals react. Having thought about our reactions, then and only then should we begin to look at our children and their responses. It is a fact that anxious mums often create anxious small miniature people who on seeing the outward signs of distress become distressed themselves, often without knowing why. These small people need reassurance. If such reassurance is not forthcoming from the parent then the child's own view of the world can be spoiled and limited.

This limitation is not about age or about development, it is about the messages that children receive from the adults nearest to them. Try to imagine the tiny baby in the pram or cradle as a receiver so complex, so clever that it is open to all and any messages. What a chastening thought that is! I cannot help but smile, recalling the gossipy conversations between young mums, overheard by small children/receivers!

When the death of someone we love happens, we often feel a variety of feelings, our emotions run high. It may be that we put off the explanation to children believing that there will be a better time. Is there ever a better time to tell a four year old that his brother is dead? A better time to explain why his daddy won't be there any more? I believe that the better time never comes and as we wait for it and as we convince ourselves that "children don't understand", we devalue and lessen the relationship we have with them.

A "gentle giant" of a man once needed to talk to me about his experiences when his brother died. He and his younger brother shared a bedroom. When he was about nine years old, he awakened during a particular summer's night. He remembered seeing his mother beside his brother's bed. In his sleepy haze he also thought that he saw his father in the room, but he was a small boy tired from a long day spent playing happily with his brother. He merely turned over and went back to sleep. When he awakened the next day, he was surprised to find that not only was his brother obviously up and about before him but that same brother had actually remembered to make his bed.

On reaching the kitchen, there was no sign of his brother. When he enquired as to where his brother was, his mother looked down at the floor and it was then he realised that she was crying and that something was very wrong. Noone explained. Before he was to go to school, neighbours and relatives came into the familiar warm kitchen and spoke in whispers whilst he, the then small, worried and anxious person longed to know what was happening and just where his brother was. A feeling of great, indescribable fear overwhelmed him. This fear grew and intensified.

When his father, who was renowned for never having missed a day's work, walked into the kitchen he knew that something was very very wrong. It was then he discovered that he was not to go to school although he knew it was a school day! This little boy actually spent the next six days with a neighbour, and kindly though she was she would not go against the wishes of the family and explain what had happened. The then boy, now the grown man, wept as he recalled those days. The days of waiting and searching for the brother whom he was never to see again. Of the kindly now embarrassed neighbour, overheard saying to her husband, believing her young charge to be out of earshot "it isn't right Tom, he should know, let me tell him". The gruff masculine reply "no it isn't for us to say anything, they must have good reason".

Whatever their reasons, kindly misguided, simple or ignorant, they, the family, the parents, have caused their son years of anguish and pain. This man who was once their own loving little boy has suffered greatly. "Why didn't they tell me?" he asked. "I could have coped with knowing he was dead. I had to when a boy at school told me that he was, but then I went back home and pretended that I didn't know because I thought that they mustn't be able to cope because they hadn't told me. It felt like a secret." He cried with me during the counselling sessions. He cried not only for himself as a man but for the special little grieving boy he was all those years ago. He shed a great many tears.

Children do need to know. Many parents seem to have the motto of closed organisations who give information to the workforce only on a "need to know" basis. Parents who decide that a child doesn't need to know then often complacently carry on with their lives believing they have done the right thing.

A young woman taking part in one of my workshops talked of how she didn't like pictures of country cottages with garden gates. She said she hated them, especially when there were children playing in the garden or standing by the gate. We talked of the work of Victorian artists who often painted children in houses and gardens and produced such works of art. "Horrible" she said, "wouldn't have one in the house". She raised her voice, it was harsh and the other people in the group noted her anger as she struggled to contain it. It was only later that she was able to talk about her real reason for disliking these pictures.

She explained that her grandma whom she loved greatly, became ill. She as a very small child watched the ailing grandma. She at five years of age was able to discern that grandma's strength was failing fast and that she had to spend longer and longer in bed. This little girl also noticed that grandma didn't have rosy cheeks any more. This same little girl noticed that grandma's skin felt different. One day on returning from school, she saw an ambulance outside her house. She knew instinctively that the ambulance had come to take grandma to hospital. Grandma had moved in with them some weeks before because she was ill. She ran into the house to find that she was right, her father explained that grandma had indeed gone to the hospital.

She wept as she told us that everyday she waited at the gate for grandma to return. Grandma never did, the weeks and months passed and you can imagine the agony of this small child waiting for this much loved grandma to return. "Where is grandma?" she would ask. "Coming soon" she would be told. Eventually she ceased to ask anymore and when in later life she asked her mother and father why they had never told her the truth, her mother replied "oh you wouldn't have understood darling, you were far too young. We did the right thing, in the end you forgot", but of course she didn't forget. That child, that little girl, now a woman, has never ever forgotten.

Children very often have a clearer perception of symbols than we adults. I find that by using symbols, children are helped to understand, even the youngest child can endeavour to see more clearly what a situation is about. In these days of hi-fi, super duper computers, technology beyond belief, it can be easy to lose sight of a child's need for simple symbols or simple magic, and yet, through all of our progress, through all of the developments and achievements within the world, from space walking to "see whose calling" phones, the tooth fairy not only persists but has now created an industry of her own.

There are special pouches and cushions in which to place the precious tooth. For almost all adults over the age of twenty-five, the tooth fairy has been a part of life. Out dropped that first milk tooth, to be placed lovingly either under the pillow or in some other secret place — ah! the effort of parents trying to prevent the child from making the place too secret without betraying the identity of the tooth fairy. "Well darling, perhaps the tooth fairy isn't used to finding little teeth inside the back of the wardrobe." The tooth fairy was and is extremely important. For many present day children she is part of the symbolism of childhood, come to think of it, she may have been a part of the symbolism of your childhood.

A man, very grumpy, once said "rubbish Mrs. Waters, I never believed in the tooth fairy". "How sad" I said, "it shows!" He grumped his way out of my company.

Having established that belief in this fairy lives on, what about the belief in small time magic? Don't we all need a bit of magic in our lives? Of course we do. We can wrap death in a little magic if we try hard enough. The mum who says "grandpa has gone to Jesus" uses the magic of religion, hoping that the child will believe that grandpa is safe, though unseen, with the friendly Jesus, still to be looked after and made safe. It is a fact that young children believe in magic if they are introduced to it at an early age.

When I want to explain to a child about death I talk about parcels and packages. I explain that our bodies are a kind of package, a kind of parcel. A very important wrapping for a very important something. Everyone of us is precious, more precious than words can ever say. The most precious part of us is inside where noone can see. It is shiny and sparkles and never dies and because it is so very precious, because it is such a treasure, we need something to keep it in so we keep it in a package. That package is called a body. Our bodies keep the shiny, precious bit safe. Sometimes packages get damaged or torn, sometimes ripped and destroyed. Eventually, the package has to go. When this happens we die but no matter what, nothing at all can destroy the precious, shiny part of us that is inside. When someone dies, the package is no use any more, it is finished. The shiny part will never be finished, it lives on and although we are not clever enough to see the shiny, precious part, this part of us rises up and soars into the sky. If you want to see where the precious part has gone, you need to look into the night sky. As you look into that sky you will see lots of shiny stars. They are really the precious parts of people. Those who don't know about this magic say they are just stars but we know that they are a shining precious part of those we love who have died.

Children cope better with knowing, especially if the knowing holds a magic explanation and if the voice that explains is full of love.

A woman in her late twenties rang me recently to tell me that she still watched the stars at night. I did not recognise her voice, she reminded me of my words and my little story that she had first heard eighteen years ago after her father died. She rang because she simply wanted me to know that she had been greatly helped by this explanation and although as an adult she had realised it couldn't possibly be true, she still felt as she looked at the stars that there was something special about them.

If you doubt that this story would actually help a child in such a situation then it would only be fair to say that there are exceptions to all rules but until you have held the warm hand of a small child and looked with him into the night sky, until you have watched the tears roll down his face as he says "goodnight daddy", until you have these experiences, you have no proof that magic doesn't work.

‘She Doesn’t Understand’

The most amazing comments are made about children. A young mother came to see me, with her she brought her one year old daughter, who spent the time we needed toddling around investigating the in’s and out’s of the furniture. Her fingers exploring the many new and interesting objects to be found in this environment new to her.

The mother was explaining how she decided to leave her husband. We talked of custody.

"What of the little one?" I ventured.

She laughed a shrill almost frightened sound.

"Oh, she doesn’t understand, she’s only one, she doesn’t need her own dad, my new boyfriend likes her, she’ll be all right."

So saying she opened her handbag and gave the child her make-up case.

"Children are very resilient" she said almost with resolution, "this guy would never hurt her."

Stepping inside the mind of a one year old is almost an impossible task. Experts do suggest that a child will or can accept parent figures per-se, but it is so easy to exercise parent power. The future of this one year old in my office is in the hands of mother, who, stops speaking to me and turns to shout at her daughter for having managed cleverly to unfasten the make-up case. The child pushes the stub of the open lipstick around her mouth. Clever stuff. She, at one, knows what the lipstick is for and yet here is the mother, together with some experts, suggesting that she will not notice that her father is gone.

How can this child understand the mum, who, having given her the make-up case to play with in the first place now scolds her because she is doing just that.

Instead of a voice which suggests she is to be rewarded for her cleverness she is now faced with a different sort of response from her mother. Here, play with this mum had said. If this child could speak surely she would now say, Hang on, you told me to play with this interesting object in the first place, I obeyed you so now how can I possibly be in trouble. Why are you shouting at me? Why don't you make up your mind. Please, please, be consistant with me.

Imagine the feelings of this child, later in life when she discovers that this inconsistant adult with whom she spends her time has made the decision that she should not spend her life with her natural daddy. She is a victim of parent power.

Thoughts on Iowa

Iowa, America.
What did I know of Iowa?
Very little, apart from the fact that it is one of the largest areas producing corn on the cob, acres and acres of it! Friends in America had told me previously that there was a whole lot of space in the state of Iowa and there I was on board a plane about to land in Des Moines airport.

It was early Sunday evening and I had travelled for hours. Tired and exhausted I almost fell out of the plane, so glad was I to have arrived at my destination.
My host came to meet me, smiling, his face full of warmth. I remembered him from the previous year when we met after one of my presentations in Chicago. Here he was again welcoming me to his beloved state with a great 'bear hug'. I had certainly arrived.

Many of us dislike goodbyes. As for me, well, I usually weep as soon as I board a return flight home or a train taking me back to my roots. Hellos are so different. They remind us who we are and are full of love and a certain anticipation. As I watched my host walk towards me I knew instinctively that I would enjoy my stay in Des Moines.

Soon we arrived at Johnne's house. He and his wife Linda recently celebrated their 40th wedding anniversary. Their home was warm and comforting but nothing could have prepared me for the appearance of a familiar box of Yorkshire tea bags sitting on the kitchen table! How this purchase had been achieved I could not guess but knowing them both as I do now no stone was left unturned to ensure that I was made to feel 'at home'.
Later I was told that Johnne had made an eighty mile round trip to get these particular tea bags. 'They are from close to your State!' he said.

This was my first experience of 'mid-west' hospitality. My friend Phyl who lives in Virginia had prepared me 'They are wonderful people in the mid-west, full of love and warmth'. This friendly couple in Iowa have a belief in God that is staggering. As they both made me welcome I realized that they would allow me to share a part of their life if only for a brief period.
One room in their house is dedicated to the bible and religious studies and it is there that Linda sits to read from the good book each day. However this couple don't just read the words, they actually act them out by leading a 'good' life, having spent years fostering children of all ages. Children who walked across the threshold of their home to be reassured, cherished and above all loved. No child turned away, always the open door of hope.
As if that were not enough each year finds one or other of them helping in some project overseas, helping those who need help of a practical nature,

and all of this atop of the love and support they provide for their own family, children and grandchildren together with the in-laws.

Why am I writing about them? It is because they practice such empathy with everyone they meet that they deserve a mention. They are an example to us all. I found that being with them was inspiring.
Linda is a nurse, again a caring profession, whilst Johnne as a financial advisor asks God daily to bless his work.
During my stay they took me to their church. They didn't insist that I go. The suggestion was mine. I wanted to leave myself open to as many new experiences as possible. Whilst in the church I listened as men and women, in appearance ordinary people, stood up and talked about the way they had exchanged most of their worldly goods for a more arduous life dedicated to God. Leaving the country of their birth they had travelled afar as missionaries, building not only churches and hospitals but improving the water supplies to villages, mending and repairing leaking roofs, often involving hard manual labour. As each couple stood before the congregation and spoke of their work their eyes shone with a brightness, indefinable but never-the-less visually discernable. It was an amazing experience for me and one that I would not have missed for the world. Very humbling, in fact.

When I returned home I was asked how I had enjoyed my stay in Iowa. One evening whilst after dinner speaking I mentioned my experience with a couple when a man in the audience rudely said 'Oh you've been with the 'God-squad'!' He then roared with laughter. Silently I looked at him and after a long pause I said that yes that was exactly where I had been and although not a fully fledged member myself I felt respect for those who were. He did not speak again.
My travels in the States have given me the opportunity to meet with a vast array of people. As many of you will know a country so large provides the visitor with a wealth of challenging situations fully enriching your experience if you want to be a part of the American way of life.

During that same visit I got to sit on the very bar stool that Clint Eastwood used during the filming of 'The Bridges of Madison County'. The diner is still there with all its memorabilia reminding people that the movie was filmed in that small township where John Wayne was born.
My host also ensured that I got to visit a patchwork shop where quilting specialists spoke with deep ardour about their craft. All in all I have to agree with the friend who long before I envisaged ever visiting the mid west told me that I would find the people there full of warmth and love. How right she was. I could have stayed much longer but had a tour which would take me to several States signing books so very reluctantly I had to leave.

During my short stay I spoke at a country club dinner to an audience so warm and friendly that at one point I was moved to tears. Good manners and courtesy abound and I felt cherished by those I met. During the book signing people told me briefly a little of their lives, one lady hoped that I would stay and see as much of the countryside as possible. Born locally she told me that it was the very best place in the world to be.

One day a very caring young woman took me to a local department store. It was getting close to Christmas and one whole floor was devoted to festive decorations. I chose one present each for all the 'girls' in my family. The shop assistant, on learning that I came from England, said that it would be her pleasure to giftwrap every chosen trinket. Whilst she did this we visited another department where I suddenly realised that once the packages were sealed I would not know which was which and all this after I had chosen so carefully for each of the girls.

My companion assured me that I need not worry, all would be well.

She was right; when we returned to collect the gifts each was beautifully wrapped with a 'post-it' note explaining what was contained within.

All too soon it was time to leave for the next venue. I was sad to say goodbye and I long to return. Johnne and Linda keep in touch and I know that they remember me in their prayers, quite a privilege I feel.

Who is the one who ne'er finds fault
Who never seeks to blame
To who we go when trouble comes
Whose love remains the same
... your mother

Two Brothers

Two men, arms outstretched, call to the camera crew for help. Two brothers trapped in the attic of their own home above the water line. Beneath them, swaying gently above the rippling floodwater, hangs the body of their mother in a makeshift sheeted hammock. 'We could not leave without her, she is our mother.'

The place is New Orleans, the year was 2005. Without the media we would not know of these men or the dozens of other true happenings. Bravely the reporting teams go to places we would not wish to see in such circumstances, and as we watch the images on our screens we feel reassured that this tragedy is not our own. But who could not be moved at the plight of these people. It was announced that force would be used to take those surviving in their homes to safety. Danger of disease and death a daily risk, still they cling on to their few belongings knowing that the world beyond holds no security for them.
Words like rescue and safety rest lightly on the ether as one woman shouted 'I am not a victim, I am a survivor'.

Often we can be critical of the press. Over the years, especially when working with the families of murder victims, I have wished that the media were not so tenacious in their pursuit of the truth but when it comes to keeping us informed we would know nothing without the reports from journalists who are actually there enabling us to see, through their eyes, the devastation. Watching the faces alone tells us so much; few journalists have been totally dry eyed when faced with disasters and deep human suffering and indeed many have lost their lives in gathering the news. Unsung heroes; the camera rarely lies.

When the film 'The Deer Hunter' was produced the critics were adamant that the American public would actually fail to visit cinemas to see it. 'The people of America see this sort of thing every day on the twenty four hour news; why would they want to pay to see details of the brutality of the war in Vietnam. Most of them have already lost someone in the war; this film will be a box office flop'.
Of course we all know that it wasn't.

On the night of its first showing, the producer and director were very worried. Perhaps the critics were correct. They would lose all the money they had invested in its production. Together they talked and, peeping into the auditorium, they could detect no response. They feared that the film would fail and shrugged their shoulders. Then they heard it, a sound, hard to recognize and yet somehow familiar. A sound we all know. They realised that people were crying. Audibly sobbing, women dabbing at tearstained cheeks, men's heads bent as they tried to locate handkerchiefs. Men and women unashamedly were crying.

The film was not a flop. The people did not feel that it was just another brutal news item. This portrayal of war reached into their hearts. They were still open to their own feelings, the Vietnam War had not brutalised them completely. Although emotionally 'punch drunk' by years of news flashes from across the world they were still capable of feeling empathy for the characters in the story. When the screening stopped no one moved. The members of the audience were so deeply affected by this wonderful visual insight that they obviously felt unable to simply get up and leave.

Who could not be moved by the plight of the people in New Orleans, people who have lost everything? Doesn't it make you feel that we should be grateful for what we have?
Within ourselves we can find compassion.
The people who bring us our news through the media are another facet of our lives. We need to know, to be informed. Without that information we could become parochial and inward looking. We need always to be aware, to allow ourselves to respond to the pain of others.
The people who have survived this tragedy could be us. They are other human beings brutally affected by the force of nature, over which we have so little control.

Two men with outstretched hands call from the attic window of the house they shared with their mother. They need help, it is their mother who hangs in the makeshift hammock below their feet.

They call to the camera crew, who do rescue them, but really they call to us, to you and to me.

Hold fast to dreams for if dreams die

Life is a broken winged bird that cannot fly

Strong Tea and Biscuits

Clover, my daughter's Airedale dog, stirred at the top of the stairs, snuffled outside the bedroom door and became restless.
It was already light, the sunshine streamed in at the window.
What time is it? I picked up the alarm clock, five a.m.! Clover, you have to be joking, this is too early even for you.

Turning over onto my side I tried to re-enter the land of nod.
But the dog was having none of it, very soon the snuffling stopped only to be replaced by a long drawn out growl. In a harsh whisper I said 'Go back to sleep you silly mutt, it's Saturday and we are having a lie in until at least seven so shush!'
Silence followed but it didn't last long. I heard the unmistakable sound of the dog making her way downstairs, and once in the hall she began to bark very loudly. As I grabbed my dressing gown I heard my daughter on the landing. 'What's wrong?' Then from halfway down the stairs 'Mum, there is someone at the door!'
'At this time? It's five o'clock in the morning.'
Having spent my life 'on call' I wondered if perhaps the phones were out of order, that this was a 'call-out' and I would find a police officer at the door.

My daughter held on to her much beloved pet who, by this time, was barking so loudly that the

occupants of the whole road could have heard. I gingerly opened the door.
At that time we were living in an old Victorian house with a huge, heavy front door which was flanked by three stone steps. Sitting on the bottom step with his head in his hands was a man. We could hear the sound of his sobbing. Unrecognizable from the back, wearing a pinstriped shirt much in need of ironing and suit trousers, no sign of a jacket, no car on the drive, nothing.
'Hello' I said.
The man looked up and turned to face us. It was then I saw that he was wearing a pair of very shabby trainers on his feet. By now my daughter, fearing for my safety, had managed to get the dog to stop barking and had positioned herself beside me in the doorway as if to indicate 'No one is going to hurt my mum!'

His cheeks were tearstained and, like a small boy, he tried to wipe his face with the back of his hand.
'I'm sorry' he said. 'I didn't know where else to go. You won't remember me but I came to see you about five years ago.'
As he spoke my 'work-head' slotted into place and I did remember him although his name escaped me.
'Sorry, I can't recall your name. It will come back to me, something to do with music. I remember you play the piano.'
His crumpled worried tear stained face showed surprise, 'What a memory!'
'Come on in, we'd best put the kettle on'.

That is exactly what we did on that lovely morning in late May. Now, nearly twenty years later, I can remember every detail of that amazing morning.
I realized that his shirt was not only crumpled but dirty. He told me later that he had been lying across the bottom step since two a.m. 'I felt desperate, didn't know what else to do. I've been trying to pluck up the courage to telephone you for almost a month ever since it happened.'

Mothers of teenage sons can often be relied upon to find spare clean shirts hanging in wardrobes waiting for the possible return of their owners. The man had a wash and was soon feeling a bit more comfortable wearing a clean borrowed shirt. A new comb sorted out his tousled hair and once in my library he settled down into the leather wing back chair with a deep, meaningful sigh.
'I need to get dressed' I said, inwardly thinking that rarely do I see people professionally whilst wearing my somewhat far from glamorous dressing gown.
'Thank you'. His voice was almost a whisper. 'I am so sorry I disturbed you'.

My daughter by this time had the tray ready. Two china cups and saucers, fresh tea in the pot and a plate of biscuits. From being very small she had watched as clients came and went from the house. Like her brothers, for her the 'tray-drill' was a matter of course.
It is amazing how quickly one can wash and dress when faced with an emergency. Within minutes I

was back in the library as my daughter and the dog prepared for an earlier than expected start to the day.

The man's name was Robert. He was, indeed, a musician. A pianist of considerable talent, a teacher of music, a man to whom music meant almost as much as life itself. But on that particular May morning he felt far from musical.
'I don't care if I never play again. I hate it all.'
Pouring him another cup of tea I said nothing. *It is not necessary in life to fill every waking moment with speech and when we are at a low ebb it can be the absence of words that proves to be most healing.*
Hugging the warm cup in both hands he stared into the tea.
'Just like before, nothing here has changed, it's still strong tea and biscuits' and then he began to cry.
He sobbed as I took the cup from his shaking hands. He sobbed as I passed him the box of tissues; he rocked and rocked as a child cries when it feels totally abandoned and alone.
Eventually the tears began to cease their flow; he stopped rocking and finally agreed to start at the very beginning. Through all of this I said nothing. Inappropriate words can do more harm than good.

He was afraid that he was about to lose his job as a music teacher, and had been asked to leave. A few weeks before he returned to his church to play the organ. 'Until all this business is sorted out', the vicar had said. 'After all, it's your word against hers.' Obviously at this point I had no idea what 'this business' was, but remembered that we need to relate our stories at our own speed in our own words.

His story came out in fits and starts, but soon it became clear that he had been accused of not only having an affair with a much younger woman in the parish but of having threatened her. It was a sorry tale. Robert told me that morning how he wanted to die. He talked of suicide, of ending his life, how by having the courage to do this he could safeguard his wife and family. Then he spoke of them with such love and warmth.

Finding the truth is about asking the right questions in a particular way and as the time passed on that day I became more than ever convinced that this man was telling the truth, that he was indeed innocent.

At around six thirty I telephoned his wife. He was once more in tears. The phone at the other end was picked up as soon it rang for the first time. Poor woman, she was beside herself with worry.

I reassured her, asking that she give me her trust. She remembered our meeting years before and felt so relieved that her husband was alive and not in the accident and emergency department of the local hospital. He was with me. Her mind was beset with doubt but deep down she knew that her husband needed her support. They had to fight this problem together.

By eight thirty she had taken the children to her mother's house, and then we heard the car draw onto our drive.

Coming into the room she flung her arms around her husband.
'I've been so worried darling. Where's your car, it's not outside. You've no jacket, that's not your shirt....Robert!'
Robert had no idea where his car was. It was found later over two miles away from my house. He was so distraught; he had reached breaking point and remembered little of the hours before we finally found him on the doorstep.
'I had to get to you Vera' he said. 'No track of time, got lost a few times I think, and then it was such a relief to just lie on the doorstep until you wakened up. I just needed to feel safe.'
As he spoke his wife, kneeling beside him, said
'Darling, we can get through this. People who know you realize that it isn't true. Not everyone believes her and as for the vicar he's just watching his own back.'
She looked into his face, smoothed his hair.

I will never forget the scene, there was so much love in their faces. They needed to be alone, somewhere safe, so that they could decide what to do....together.
'Would you like a cup of tea?' I asked her.
'Yes, please' she nodded, eyes brim full.
Before I left the room to go into the kitchen I crouched down in front of them both. 'Robert, shall I bring in strong tea and biscuits?'
'Please' he smiled for the first time that day.
'Just like always', he said.
'Last night was the longest night of my life'.

Having placed the replenished tray on the table beside them I suggested that they relax for a while and on my return we would consider the next positive step in their lives. They needed time to be together, undisturbed. My presence was not required, at least for the next hour or so.

Life in the house around them continued, it was Saturday and there were the usual chores. My daughter and I had things we needed to do. Before we left to go shopping I knocked gently at the door of the library, popped my head around and asked the couple if they would close the front door when they left.

'You are welcome to sit in the garden, it is a lovely day after all. You can get in touch with me whenever you want, but now I think that you need special time together. You are quite safe here. Feel free to put the kettle on and there are more biscuits in the biscuit barrel'. Sometimes in our lives we need to be in a place of safety; simply to catch our breath, to breathe deeply, feeling safe and loved. We provide sanctuaries for birds and animals, we humans need them too.

Ten days later the young woman who had accused Robert admitted that nothing had happened. She had been dared by two friends to accuse this caring family man, 'it was just a joke' she told the police. A joke! A prank that almost took a man's life away and could have destroyed his family!

There are times in our lives when we feel that we are at the lowest ebb. No matter how we try we cannot see the light at the end of the tunnel. Standing on the edge of quiet desperation we do not know where to go or to whom to turn. That feeling of isolation can border on despair.

Robert and his wife eventually gathered the remnants of their life together. It was not easy but love and a belief in one another can prove to be much stronger than some of the awful experiences that we face during our lives.

A red faced vicar invited Robert to return as the organist at the church, trying to dismiss his own behaviour as 'Well, you see I couldn't take any chances and it's not as though for one moment I doubted you', but Robert refused, with a sad look on his face.

The young woman's parents did not know what to do, they felt so ashamed. Their daughter still lived at home and within a few months the family had left the district, never to be seen again.

Robert and his wife stayed in my life for quite a time until they felt ready to stand alone. As we said our last goodbyes, always a moving experience for me, they gave me a present.

Opening the box I found nestling amidst bright pink tissue a lovely china cup and saucer, a packet of tea bags and a tin of biscuits. Much later that day, long after they were gone, I found a small card that had slipped between the layers of paper on which was written

'With our thanks and love, tea and biscuits for you to share with others'.

When my eldest son came up with the idea of a title for this book I smiled as I immediately remembered Robert and his lovely wife and that sunny May morning all those years ago. The other day, whilst being interviewed, I was asked how many people I had coached or counselled during my career. Of course it is impossible to answer that question. I didn't tell the journalist about the number of times that I discovered clients sitting in my garden, standing in my greenhouse or waiting in parked cars across the road, on the drive or, like Robert, lying on the front doorstep. There is a great need for peace in all of our lives. When we become distressed and anxious we often gravitate towards someone or some place that can lead us to that peace of mind.

Love is much stronger than hate, much more durable. It can be unconditional, everlasting, brief or even momentary. It can take many forms, including the provision of sanctuary for a friend.

On the kitchen wall above my electric kettle is a metal sign. It was a present from Maggs, who once played an important part in the working team. It is a copy of one of those stirring, reassuring, encouraging messages put out during World War Two. Messages to help keep up the morale of a nation at war. The sign says: WAR DEPT.WHEN IN DOUBT BREW UP!

As my son reminds me, everyone who has ever come to see me whether professionally or as a friend is always offered

'Strong tea and biscuits'......

I rest my case.

Do not stand at my grave and weep

I am not there; I do not sleep.

I am a thousand winds that blow,

I am the diamond glints on snow

I am the sun on ripened grain

I am the gentle autumn rain

When you awaken in the morning's hush

I am the swift uplifting rush

Of quiet birds in circling flight.

I am the soft starlight at night

Do not stand at my grave and cry,

I am not there; I did not die

Mary Frye

The Grave

The two small pieces of amethyst felt smooth to the touch. They nestled in the pocket of my jacket as I sat in the plane on my way to Berlin. Asked to provide training for senior managers in an airline company I felt that yet another adventure was coming on. It is always good to be visiting new places and other countries, especially this one. Germany is a place of progressive thinking that hides within itself harsh memories of a painful and somewhat shameful past.

'What will it be like?' I asked myself. 'Will I like the Germans?' After all we were once at war with them. I thought of the last years of the Second World War, of sitting on my father's knee at the cinema watching the Pathe News. Putting my fingers in my ears and hoping that someone would come onto the screen and sing happy songs.
'What is a war, daddy?'

'It's a time when men have to go away and fight for their country'.
'Will you go daddy?'
'No, you know I work at the steel works. The soldiers need steel for weapons to fight the jerrys. I do my bit here in the home guard.'
'What are jerrys?'
'The Germans'.
'Oh' I said as my mother told both of us to be quiet.

The plane bumped into cotton wool clouds, the seatbelt signs went on as I became more excited than ever to be visiting Berlin.

Closing my eyes several pictures came into my mind. Many of them the faces of men, once my clients, who were referred to me simply because they had become institutionalised after years in mental hospitals. They had fought for King and Country but on returning home had no place to live and no chance of work. Post Traumatic Stress Disorder, no one had heard of that. Shell shock eventually was to become the acceptable terminology. As they failed to adjust they were labelled and simply 'put away'. It was all so simple. Years later I sat with them listening as they recounted the horrors of war. Often they cried, mourning for the lives lost, also grieving for their own lost lives.

Life for these survivors in the late 1940's, early 1950's, became another sort of hell. As the plane continued on its way I could still hear once more the cracked and pitch less voice of a man singing 'Old soldiers never die... they simply fade away' as a nurse led him away, back to the ward.

'No use talking to him' said a young member of staff. 'He has been bonkers for years.'

I remember standing up, blocking the exit to the room, facing the two men, one a patient, too old to continue to fight, the second a carer, too young to acknowledge what the fight was about.

'But for him you could have been subject to a curfew.'
'A what?' A bemused look.
Looking out of the window I realised we were coming into land. So many trees, huge wide avenues lined with trees and then suddenly the colour green stopped. Looking down I realised that only half of this city was tree lined, the rest was bare.

Later walking through the streets I experienced an overwhelming feeling of 'déjà vu.' It was as though I knew the place, I felt its pain. Looking out from the third floor window of the apartment from which I was to stay I noticed bullet holes peppering the walls of the older buildings across the street. It was as though I had been in that same place at some other time. The feeling of knowing continued and intensified, there was no explanation, no reason, it was simply how I felt. Inexplicable.
All in my mind I thought or was it? A few days later as I walked in the sunlight on a busy street I reminded myself quite sternly that I had never ever visited this city previously. Think positively, I told myself, however the feeling persisted and returns.... whenever I set foot in the city of Berlin, there was much to see during that first visit.
Accompanied by a close friend I visited the military cemetery. There was a stillness as we walked between the rows of graves. Neither of us

spoke. A couple of people wandered among the white crosses. No one else came in through the gates, we remained undisturbed. So absorbed were we that over an hour passed, the time seemed to fly, then with surprise we called one to the other that it was time to move on.

Just at that moment I looked at the words on the grave at my feet.

'Look at this. This plane went down right at the very end of the war, how unlucky. All the crew were killed.'

I remarked 'What a terrible waste of young lives.' It was during the Berlin Airlift, how sad.

Putting my hand in the pocket of my jacket I took out one of the small pieces of polished amethyst. Placing it on the outstretched wooden arm of the cross I said "This is just for you, I was a baby when you died, thank you so much for my freedom." With that we left.

Weeks later whilst at the hairdressers I mentioned that I had been to Germany. The salon was full of eager customers so there was only a limited time to speak.

'I'd like to go there,' Wendy, the owner said. 'I lost my dad right at the end of the war.'
'Berlin is a lovely city, you should try to visit.'

No more was said and the conversation was forgotten.

Many months past. Unbeknown to me Wendy made plans to visit Berlin. Whilst she was away her husband came to see me.
We were enjoying a cup of tea when his mobile phone rang.
Hello he said and then mouthed to me that it was Wendy telephoning from Germany. Before he could say another word his wife said 'I found my Dad's grave today, it's good to know at last where he is laid to rest. I am so glad I came here. Oh, and by the way, Vera has been here.'
'How do you know?'
There is a piece of amethyst on the grave. I know that it is from her.'

Geoff finished the call and told me the details of the conversation. You see it was true, out of all the graves I could have chosen it was that particular place, that one cross amidst the many crosses that attracted my attention What was more surprising was the fact that I had never known Wendy's maiden name, not being from the locality in which I now live my friendships here are fairly recent.

Was it all a coincidence or as the old song says, 'just one of those things'? Amazing thing coincidence, but then life is full of happenings that despite all our learning and wisdom cannot be explained. Usually we say, often with a wry smile,

'It was just a coincidence'. But was it?....Really? I am never quite sure.
Three years ago I visited Australia. I was excited at the prospect of visiting a country so far away. I longed to see it all but was scheduled to visit Perth and Sydney where I was to speak I was to give a three hour lecture to senior Police officers followed by a series of broadcasts on the radio. A dear friend accompanied me on the trip. We both found Perth to be a beautiful city with lots to see.

Books have always held a fascination for me. I simply cannot walk past the door of an inviting bookshop without popping in. Australia was no exception. Their bookshops were more intriguing still as so many of them were swap shops. Exchanging one book for another after the payment of a small fee. How simple, almost a fee paying library. Wanting to know more I walked into one of these obviously interesting places to see a tall man with a distinctive profile rummaging about on one of the shelves. Surely not the owner I thought as I noticed his tattered jeans and much faded shirt. But he was the owner. Very soon he disappeared through a doorway at the back of the counter. That proved it. Would I ever get used to the total lack of dress code in this country?

Eventually he reappeared. His name was Colin. He was not only genial but incredibly charming. He asked if I came from Yorkshire, first explaining that he had married a Yorkshire lass years before. 'Wrong rose' I said.

'Not white then.'
'No, red. I'm a lassie from Lancashire'. We laughed together.
'You must meet Cynthia' he said 'she will be so pleased to talk with someone from back home.'

We arranged that I would return after visiting Sydney to meet his wife Cynthia. Six days later I did. She looked at me strangely then said "You don't remember me, Vera Phillips, do you?" It was a long time since anyone had called me by my previous married name. Surprised, I agreed that although I did not recognise her there was something about her that seemed familiar. It was strange, but I couldn't quite put my finger on it! How strange. She poured me a glass of bottled water, offered me a biscuit and then said 'Wait a minute, this will surprise you, I will tell you where we met. It was in the seventies, you were holding an awareness workshop in London. You were one of the National Trainers for the Health Service and I was one of the mature students who spent three days with you!'
That course was unforgettable. I still have the notes at home after all these years.
'You've changed, Vera, but I would know that voice anywhere!'
Small world or coincidence, whatever, it takes some explaining.
I was even more surprised when a few days later this lady showed me the notes from that original residential course. Unbelievably she had kept them for over 25 years. I had travelled thousands

of miles only to find someone who knew me and remembered the work we had done together. Before I returned home I met with them several times, the simple coincidence somehow brought us closer together. Simple did I say, probably an understatement!!
We were all gripped by the unexpected chain of events that brought us together.

Coincidence, or simply something that we cannot explain. Something that happens without reason, something for which we as mere human beings do not have an explanation.
Constantly I am reminded that on the one hand we must try to take control of our lives and that we do have choices then, on the other hand, something inexplicable occurs and we are rendered momentarily speechless. However we do not have to let this put us off from seizing our life with all its opportunities. Surely these quirks of coincidence are encouraging reminders that there is so much to learn. Our whole life can be a constant learning curve if only we can find the courage to leave ourselves open to the experience.
I cannot explain why I left the amethyst on that particular grave in Berlin or why whilst in Australia I met a woman who had heard me lecture over two decades before or why she had kept the programme for all those years. But although the experience momentarily caused 'goose-bumps' on the back of my neck I find that every time I recall these so called coincidences I am filled with excitement.

Try looking back on your life. Rethink those happenings that you put down to coincidence. Relive them, whilst at the same time reminding yourself that yes there is so much in the world that we have yet to learn. Make today a step on your journey to heightened awareness.

Men must be taught as if you taught them not

And things unknown proposed as things forgot

Alexander Pope 1688-1744

The Workplace

This book would be incomplete without a visit to the workplace. Being retained by various companies and organizations has meant that I have spent a great deal of my time looking at the way we affect each other especially whilst at work.

In our private lives we stand a much better chance of being loved, whilst at work we spend our time with people who were once strangers and who do not necessarily become friends. Only the work, payment and the need to be industriously employed is all that initially binds us together. That linkage is tenuous, therefore easily destroyed.

Some companies are highly successful. Others flounder. Is it all down to the stock market? I hardly think that it is as simple as that. If only it were. The solutions would then be very distinct, black or white, no shades of grey!
Imagine a huge patchwork quilt, life itself! We are all part of that giant fabric.

Now look at the quilt closer, what do you see? Millions of tiny patches, each representing a person. The colour, texture and pattern of each piece or patch is different. No two pieces are identical. There are spots, stripes, floral designs, abstract patterns and plain colours, some vibrant and highly coloured, others pale and almost nondescript but all are part of the whole finished piece.

There are very complex ways to describe the ways in which our personality and thinking work, the ways in which these two aspects of our very being combine together. However I have no wish to bore you with complexity. At any given time we are responding from one of three standpoints. The child, the adult and the parent. Let us simplify the process by looking in the work-place. Fly on the wall documentaries have become very popular, the following is a story changed slightly to preserve confidentiality. It is a story of everyday behaviour in the work place. The names and events have been cosmetically fictionalised but never-the-less this is a TRUE account!

Dennis's Story.

Dennis worked in a factory. Every day he stood by his machine doing a boring and repetitive job. He did not enjoy the work, he did not consider himself to be clever or educated. At an early age he had worked out that people like him led hum-drum lives and at least he was in full time employment.
The wage was reasonable, enough to live on. He smoked and enjoyed a pint in the pub a couple of times a week. Dennis knew who he was, where he was, and that he found comforting. He could often be heard remarking that he had no wish to change his life. He obtained comfort in the familiarity of the factory and prided himself on knowing every

nook and cranny. He also knew about the little scams that certain people involved themselves in. 'More fool them' he said under his breath. He was aware of all the gossip. Who fancied Julie in the office for instance and who found the wages clerk difficult to deal with. All of this gave Dennis the comfort zone he needed to work in, the comfort of knowing about things and in knowing he had areas of control.

Dennis had read recently that 'knowledge was power', well he had his own sort of 'knowledge'. He smiled, fancy calling that power - 'it's the bosses that have all the power!'

On more than one occasion he had been asked to become the shop steward for the union. He did not want that. That sort of responsibility would get in the way of his routine. If he took that position he would have to do something about the problems that fellow employees brought to him. Everything would get out of order.

Things are best left as they are thought Dennis.

This man did not constantly enjoy his work but he made the work situation fit around him, he accepted his limitations and lived by them.

He had knowledge, therefore he had a power of sorts although he did not see himself in this way. This allowed Dennis to function in a very ADULT way for a large proportion of the time he was in the workplace.

Then suddenly on a sunny day, without a hint of warning, Dennis's life changed completely. The factory manager did not come into work at the usual time. A punctual man by nature he was never ever late.

Whispering started between the operatives on the machines. One girl, always very full of herself with a great deal to say, declared that she would go and 'chat up Ted in the office and see what was going on'.

The 'chatting up' must have taken longer than she thought and when she came back down onto the shop-floor she was white.

'Lost yer touch' called one of the women at the far end.
'Shut up' the girl said, 'ee's dead.'
'Yer joking, 'ee can't be, 'ee was alright yesterday.'
Obviously the man had not been totally alright.

Suddenly Dennis's life stopped being alright. The management lost no time in replacing the dead man with a new man and within days he had a nickname - Eager Beaver!

Slick, knowledgeable, marketplace orientated. A different sort of manager. Not 'hands-on'. He lost no time in making them aware that he was in charge and they were 'his' workers.

Dennis's comfort zone began to crumble. It began in small ways. This new man TOLD everyone what to do and when. His predecessor had always spoken

with respect to the workers although everyone knew that when he wanted a job done, it got done, otherwise you were in trouble.
This new man had obviously never ASKED for a job to be done. He gave out commands and saw himself as a cut above the workers in the various sections of the shop floor. He constantly bossed people about. Ripples of unrest spread through the place. Dennis described how he felt to his wife. When at home he rarely spoke about work but his wife of over thirty years, knowing him so well, realised that something was wrong.
'He talks to us as though we are kids, stupid kids at that.'
'Frank says he feels like punching 'im in the face.'
'That won't get him far with you lot.'
'He'll learn the hard way', concluded Dennis.

Neither Dennis nor his colleagues had studied psychology but they had been part of the University of Life; they were full of common sense!

This story has a happy ending. The new manager was replaced. As he left he said 'Well, it wasn't good enough for me anyway!' He marched out of the owner's office like a naughty child, slamming the door in his wake.

If you want to show another human being respect, remember that they need to be in the ADULT part of their personality to respond with logic. If you want to get the best out of people in your life, making them feel small achieves nothing. Dennis liked the next manager. There was no messing him about. Everyone knew that!

Working in the corner, Arnold, another man of a few words said, 'I wouldn't like to cross him but he's fair enough!'

Sometimes when work fell behind the new man did let them see who was the boss....as if they didn't know! Then he definitely sounded like a parent but that wasn't often as they usually worked hard.
Dennis liked the way the new man commented when a job was done well and of late Dennis had started giving him some advice. He took it.
'Got his head screwed on right' said Dennis.
None of us enjoy being made to look small. When someone talks to us as though we know nothing, as if we are inefficient, or just plain dumb, there is no place to go within ourselves.

Most of us respond to praise and appreciation.
We need the understanding and empathy of other people.........
Why?
The answer is simple.....
WE are human beings.

On Being Jilted

Jilted. A good old fashioned word jilted, it apparently comes from way back in history. One dictionary definition says "to cast off (a lover) after encouraging." Well, that certainly is an apt description of what jilting is all about.

Some people live alone, never linking up to another to create a larger unit. Often they admit that they feel happiest in their own company. By being able to cope with yourself, without another, is for many an exercise in self discipline. However we can so easily be cast into the Alone state quite abruptly with cries of 'oh I never knew!'

Our society in its very patterns still leads the young and up and coming teenager to believe that coupling is not only the norm but a necessity. One thing is certain. If you have spent a period of your life wrapped in the love of another human being, if you have shared home and possessions then to lose that person suddenly can fill you with total and utter grief. The whole experience turns us from a logical adult into a crying child. Still the propaganda continues and, as ever, the young person in our society believes that falling in love is an essential part of life's rich pattern.

If death were the thief that robbed us of the one we loved then we can woefully and acceptingly mourn. Other people can see our grieving. They send gestures of thoughtfulness and empathy, flowers and cards arrive and provide for us small crumbs of comfort at this most difficult of times. On being jilted there are often no cards or flowers or gestures of goodwill.

We can usually depend on the fact however that there will be much gossip and speculation, often by those who have carried the banner, the flag of friendship above their heads.

On being jilted we are left with a sense of failure. If not at the very beginning of the process, the sense of failure will come during or even after. Does time heal, it's an old adage that suggests that it does. It is my belief that time doesn't necessarily heal. What does happen is that because life has to go on we force ourselves into the next twenty four hour capsule and work through it, and in so doing use up the energy that we would need to mourn more deeply in this Alone State.

Often it is the lot of the jilted person to remain in a house full of memories. If you are that person you will find yourself sitting in the same familiar room looking at the furniture and everything that has gone to make a house into your home. Looking around you, you see a picture that you bought together. You hear again, in your mind, your shared laughter and separately the laughter of your partner. The hugs, the kisses, the joy of that day seem to surround you. From the picture you look to the rest of the room, the carpet, ah yes, the pattern that he didn't like but you did. You coerced and cajoled and insisted and here you are left with that same carpet. Upstairs the slippers still beside the bed as though waiting to remind you that your lover will not return. You know that he or she has gone never to return, usually belonging now however briefly to another, possibly with a younger person full of life and vitality whilst you, the jilted one grow older by the second.

The jilter on the other hand has places to go and people to see, clothes to buy for the new image. Not the man or woman you love but a stranger. A person who looks different yet has the same mannerisms and a familiar voice. You still love and want your partner who now speaks of other people as though he or she is a stranger and you should understand.

Nobody tells us how to cope with the pain of rejection. The anxiety that accompanies this feeling is immeasurable, the knowing that the person you love is now with another person whom they now love. All that you are left with is the emptiness and the void.

It is at these times that it seems that every song ever written seems to be about love lost, love found, love missed, love dying or love eternal. The lyrics do nothing to help support or uplift you. It is a good idea at this time to make sure you have all non vocal tapes in the car as you can be driving along and suddenly find yourself becoming tearful as a singer puts into words the very thoughts that are in your head and in your mind.

And then again there is that familiar home. In its way it can be comforting but in another way is not comforting at all, for every time you sit in that same room where you both sat together for so long your world seems full of memories. Why not break the pattern — go out and buy a new lamp, a nest of coffee tables, an ornament, a new rug, something that will stop the pattern passage of your thoughts. Yes you will still look at the picture, you will still remember the carpet and then your eyes will fall on the nest of coffee tables that you bought yourself after the parting, then you will be forced to remember that you went into a shop, on your own, and chose the tables carefully and took them home. There are no thoughts of your lover connected with those tables, only thoughts of the new you striving to survive.

If there are some particular items in your home that cause you to become emotional at the most unexpected times then put them away for a while. A great many people take down all the photographs, put them in drawers. A sense of temporary healing often accompanies this action but the tearing up of photographs should be considered carefully, especially wedding photographs because as you cut across the smiling images of the couple encaptured within the frame remember that you cut across yourself. It is a great shame to cancel out all the love that there has been. In that lovely song from "Chess" sung by Elaine Page and Barbara Dickson there is a line that says "No one is completely on your side. Would we love them if they were?"

As in most other kinds of grieving process caused by whatever reason, the double bed when occupied by one person becomes an arid desert of loneliness. Where once when going early to bed we had luxuriated in the fact that we could stretch our legs and arms to the four points of the double or king size bed now we want only to touch the person who shared it with us, but they are there no longer.

It is a fact that after being jilted many people experience great difficulty in going to sleep. Take a pillow and lay it where your partner would have been, you will find that during the night your arm will go round the pillow and you will comfort yourself, making the bed seem less empty than it really is. As the days go by and form themselves into weeks try new recipes, make meals that you have not shared with the person who has now gone, try new ideas. If you can afford it, or do it yourself, change the decoration in the lounge or bedroom, make something in your home different so that you too can grow with that change and having done this then look in your wardrobe and ask yourself is it time for you to look different, is it time for you to look at having a new image even though there is no one new in your life, no princess for the glass slipper, no prince charming to steal you away.

It is worth remembering at such times that in order for another door to open we have to have doors that close in our life. It sounds like a cliché to say that as one door opens another one closes but isn't that exactly what happens in so many instances? If, at this moment you have been recently rejected, you will not believe as you read these words that you will have a new life. Yet look around, there are people whom you know have had this experience and who are now happily in relationships with other people. The greatest difficulty with being jilted is the fact that it saps the confidence so badly that it makes us feel as though we are not only unworthy but unlovable. We start to grow when we realise that no relationship is really one hundred percent safe and that if our partner leaves us, albeit for another, we have to eventually get to the point where we accept that if the relationship had been a hundred percent then our partner would not be with someone else. It is easy to neglect a relationship, to get it wrong, to forget that dotting the i's, crossing the t's is an important part of making a lasting relationship. The thoughtfulness, the kindness and the support, remain long after the loving lust is gone.

When you have cried for what seems like forever, when you have hidden away and not dared to go out, when you have drunk yourself silly, when you have eaten yourself sick, when you have starved yourself and lost weight, when you have done any or all of these things then it is time to start anew. Painstakingly and carefully compile a list of your likes and dislikes, these are your preferences, they are about you as a single person and not as part of a pair. Even the most simple questions at this time in your life are capable of making you feel incredibly sad. Write the answers anyway and when you have finished read through your list. Preface what you read with the words "I am a person who likes the colour red, enjoys music by the Beatles, goes fishing, jogging, likes to read about golf, hates very hot weather" and so on and so forth.

You might easily feel at this point that nothing would be gained by doing this but the discipline that will keep you in one piece, in one functioning piece, has to start somewhere. It starts in small ways when we take part of ourselves to ourselves and exert some control. Before you can cope fully with the knowledge that you have been jilted you need to know who the person was, who fits into that category, you are well aware that you know the person who went off and did the dirty deed, but you need to know what kind of a person he or she left behind. Oh, and by the way, it isn't a good idea to step right into the market place, to do yourself up like a dog's dinner and to go out and actively look for another partner. Remember the logic in your personality is found within the adult part of your thinking. When we are bereaved, sad, jilted, anxious and don't know where to turn, it is the child in us that functions at the highest level. Our child has little or no logic. If we go into the market place too early then we will find ourselves in a bigger mess then ever, with someone we don't really like who just momentarily showed us a little kindness and consideration. To go too early into the market place is to take with us an invisible begging bowl. We carry it before us saying mutely "I am hurt, rejected and confused, please love me." Some people, although still carrying the bowl and giving the same message, decide to put on a brave outward face and go into a pattern of going out with other people merely to get even with the opposite gender.

Our society doesn't help when it comes to getting on with life without a partner. Suddenly a woman who has had many friends safe within relationships of their own finds herself without so many friends. Overnight she has become the 'femme fatale,' she doesn't feel any differently but certain of her friends view her now as a single woman obviously on the look out for another man. Men are often wooed by dinner party hosts, neighbours, people who have friends who are single, in other words the matchmaking begins. Often the rejected man does not want to be part of this scene at all and as for the femme fatale, well curled up at home in an empty overlarge double bed, she wonders how mistaken everyone can be.

If you have never been to the cinema or sat in a restaurant on your own, paid a bill, signed a cheque or simply taken responsibility for what goes on in the administrative side of your home, then losing your partner can cause tremendous upheaval and problems. Without the respectability of the widow's weeds help can be very slow at coming! It is at this time that many people wish they had learned to be more independent, to do more, to be more confident as in the case of a woman fitting a plug. To be able as a man to choose your own clothes and to know that they look right. The Alone State zaps our emotional confidence, suggesting to us that we can't cope. Remember that you can. It is a good idea to stay out of the limelight, even to steel yourself into the self discipline that keeps you away from friends just for a short while. Remember that whilst you are talking in detail to a so called friend about the ins and outs of your broken relationship, you may well be telling more than one person. The lives of others can become very very interesting even if in fact the listener's life has very little in it that one could call scintillating. The estranged couple become like a pair of actors on a stage, their friends often an over participatory audience who give not only advice but firm controlling suggestions.

Try taking small steps, one at a time. The goal for one week could be actually doing something on your own that you haven't done before; for a second week it could be about changing something in the house, and for the third week changing something about your appearance. Set your goals, work to them, try not to be too downhearted if you don't reach them.

A lovely man who was once in this position described himself as feeling as though he were a small boy learning about things he should have known long ago. Having become exasperated with the inner workings of the washing machine he decided to go out and use the launderette. One visit to the launderette and he was back trying to find the booklet that told him what to do with the machine. "I have never been mechanically minded" he said, "left everything to do with household appliances to her, felt it was her job, wife, mother all of that you know but after sitting in that launderette with an inquisitorial female I felt more vulnerable than I have ever felt in my life, and the only person I wanted was my wife."

Coping with being jilted isn't easy, it never was and it never will be and it takes time to get confidence back, to look in the mirror and like the person that you see there. Remember small steps, one at a time, and as I have said earlier in this section, remember that at times of crises you need to live in twenty four hour capsules, consider yourself a successful winner as you survive one day, passing to the next, keep moving! That's the secret, keep surviving!

Try to avoid encouraging your friends, relatives and acquaintances to talk freely with you about your private life. Parts of our lives are private, yet when we are rejected or jilted these parts often become public as though everyone we know has a right to know the most gory details. Remember that with relationships people have very varied codes of pattern of behaviour. Every time we talk about the other man or the other woman we introduce them into the room in which we sit, we bring them in. They do not need to be tangibly present, they are there in our speech and in our thoughts. We are introducing them to friends who say "what's she like?" "what is he like?" "is she younger?" and so it goes on. Unless it was your idea and your ambition as a child to be an actor or actress then look at the situation carefully and you will find that that is fast what you are becoming.

Friends will allow you to be the visiting cabaret, only for as long as it suits them and then they are faced with the inevitable question of whether or not to be friendly, to continue the friendship with the jilter and the jilted. You may feel very much betrayed when a dear friend tells you that she or he is going to keep in contact with the partner who has deserted you. Not everyone can be loyal to one party. It is evident not only in the political field but in our private lives. Other people cannot cancel out the days, the weeks, the outings, the experiences they have shared with you as a couple, taking sides is very very difficult. Your partner may well have jilted you but ask yourself why. Did you do enough, did you keep the relationship young and vibrant in itself or did you neglect it, take it for granted and cease to work at it?

Because we are so dependent one upon the other we are devastated when the person we love leaves us. It is at this time once again we must try to learn to love ourselves a little more.

In many ways grieving for someone who is dead brings with it respectability. Grieving for someone who simply gets up and walks out of our lives leaves no such respectability. Instead of sympathy we are often met with criticism and cries of "I told you so." There are no flowers to cheer us and no cards to put upon the mantelpiece, to prove that other people sympathise with our sad loss. Often the garment of mourning is denied us and only those who are our true friends will continue to give us support.

However being jilted need not be the end of our life. Although during the experience we often wish that it could be so. The grieving process begins and as in all mourning experiences changes start to take place. If you make a decision to try to rebuild your life then you have taken the very first step on the positive road to recovery. You will never forget the experience, it cannot be totally forgotten, not only because of its pain content but also because it is such a difficult learning experience.

Take it as part of your life!

Name it!

Claim it!

Then throw it away!

Who knows at some time in the future when you meet a person who really cares about you, you may feel like sending a thank you card to the person who originally jilted you.

Life passes
Like a drift of silk chiffon
Slipping
Thro' the fingers of time

Vera Waters

The Fountain Pen

Blue, a beautiful shade of blue. His fountain pen was blue.
'You have to be very careful with a pen like this', he would say, 'it's a Conway Stewart, they make the best pens in the world.'
I believed him. Why wouldn't I. He was my uncle returned from the war. He had been imprisoned by the Japanese and had awful scars to prove it.
For me at five years old he was a wonderful man; I wanted to look after him to take his pain away.
'Pass me the bottle of ink, now this is the difficult bit'. He would take the lid off the ink and, after lowering the pen into the blue liquid, he pulled the little lever on the side of the pen.
'Easy does it, slow and easy.'
His hands shook. On some days he trembled so much that the ink bottle slid across the table. 'Oops' he would say on those occasions.
'Not so good today kid.'
When my Uncle James called me 'kid' I felt proud, special, as though I was a different person...
The phrase 'Not so good today kid' was a signal, a secret message between us that meant he wanted me to take on the precious task of filling the blue mottled fountain pen.
What an honour. The moment I passed him the refilled pen I was one with him, a grown up, not merely a child.
A sheet of paper would be beside the scrap of blotting paper which was part of this ritual and

having gently caressed the nib with the latter he would write his name on the paper in flowery script.
'Conway Stewart' he repeated the name with reverence, 'makers of the best pens in the world.'
Thus it was that my interest in pens began. My father, who wrote quite a lot, always liked to use a well sharpened pencil. He carried a small penknife in his inside jacket pocket for this purpose. He took it upon himself to keep me well supplied with pencils as he knew that even at that early age my story writing had begun.
'You will find a pencil quicker our Vera, much quicker; remember that your brain will work much faster than your hand can write so an ordinary pen is out of the question'. By an ordinary pen he meant a Biro. Whilst other people felt the Biro pens were wonderful my father felt that good neat or flowing script was ruined by the ball point pen.
'Pencils have always worked best for me, girl' and that was the end of it.

It was then that I began to wish for a special pen of my own. I longed for a fountain pen. I knew that my parents could well afford to buy me one, but somehow for them this particular purchase was not high on their agenda, so I continued to yearn for something I could not have.
One day my mother and I were seated in the waiting room of a railway station. The train was late, a fault on the line. The guard came to tell us that we would be delayed for at least half an hour. Apart from ourselves there was only one other

person in the room. A man was seated across from us wearing a suit and a black homburg hat exactly like the one on the shelf in my father's wardrobe. Hearing the news of the delay he sighed and took a notebook out of his attaché case followed by something else. I watched in awe as he produced a small narrow wallet containing not one pen but two.
Obviously judging by the colour the pens were not like my uncle's pen. Similar but not quite the same. They were so beautiful!
That was the day I decided that when I had enough money I would not simply buy a Conway Stewart pen in a box, but one with a little leather wallet. Closing my eyes for a moment I imagined myself sitting, just like the man, writing in a notebook. Everyone thinking that I was an author!
The dream was born, the goal was set, it was the beginning.

Years passed by. My life went on. I never quite got around to buying the dream pens. It wasn't that I lost sight of my goal, it was simply that there always seemed to be some reason why the purchase could not be justified. In my teens I became engaged to a boy I truly loved. He unfortunately was not a Catholic. High church Protestant. Our parents were all ardent churchgoers, albeit different denominations. Marriage between us was out of the question. Four adults held a meeting and it was decided that despite the small gold ring I proudly wore on my finger there would be no nuptials to follow, ever.

During one of our many troubled outings my boyfriend talked to me of what it would be like when we married, all the presents he would buy me, the house we would rent, as far away from our parents as we could.

'Those pens', he said, 'the ones you dream of, I'll buy them for you, so you can write and write.'

Write I did when he was posted to B F P O fifty six in Tobruk. National Service with its compulsory orders parted us temporarily. The ball point pen ran across the pages and pages of our daily letters until one day he received a letter telling him that I did not love him any more.

No, I did not write the letter. Its arrival with him so many miles away coincided with the strange loss of my engagement ring which suddenly disappeared. Little did we know then that the determination of the adults in our lives had sent it on its way to him as he served abroad? It arrived with him weeks later. She has found some one else his mother's letter said 'and doesn't want you any more'.

His letters stopped. He was gone from my life until I felt that it had all been a dream, my true love an illusion, but at least two sets of parents were sure that their lies and subterfuge were justified. Anything was better than a mixed marriage.

'You need a good catholic marriage' my father muttered to himself one day. As though such an arrangement was the answer to every man made problem.

My heart was broken, not knowing that all of my fiancés letters were intercepted by my parents only

to be found years later. The truth never discussed or revealed.
During that troubled period I wrote a lot of poetry, sad, full of tears and pathos.
I missed my love and suspected nothing.
My father decided he would buy me a set of Parker pens. He did not grasp or understand why I showed no gratitude and appreciation. They lay unused in the box gathering dust. Until eventually my mother removed them from my room telling me how ungrateful I was. Ironically she passed them on to my Uncle James.
He tried to persuade me to use them, to write my poems, my stories but I felt relieved to know that he had them and they were no longer in my parents' house.
The dreaded pens in their fine presentation box were not mentioned again.

Years passed. I married and had three wonderful children but no spare cash to buy expensive pens. Occasionally when waiting on a draughty cold railway station I would remember the suited man in the Homburg and remind myself that the purchase and ownership of a set of pens was one of my life's goals.
We all need goals to guide us. We need to aim towards something otherwise we become aimless, achieving very little. Often we exist or survive, unfocused, drifting from day to day.
The odd Parker pen came my way and then I read about Henry Waterman, an insurance agent in the days before the fountain pen had even been

invented. The story goes that he was about to have a client sign a very important contract, worth a great deal of money. Unfortunately the bottle of ink was empty. By the time the young Waterman had dashed down the road to purchase another bottle of ink one of his competitors had rushed in and stolen the contract. Doubtless he was carrying a spare bottle of ink!
Hence the Waterman fountain pen was invented.
As soon as I read and re-read this account I knew that it was not a Conway Stewart pen I wanted to own but a Waterman.

Beside me as I write this is a well worn, slim, leather pouch. It contains two pens. Green in colour, mottled.
They are Waterman pens.
Several years ago I achieved my goal.
A journey that had started when I was seven years old became reality when I was almost fifty years of age.
Why then?
Life threatening experiences can change our lives in more ways than one. After suffering from an illness for several months I was back at work giving presentations, meeting interesting people. It is difficult to wind down after being on stage. When we read of actors and performers they often describe the ways in which they fight the drop in adrenalin that follows the heightened state needed to perform. After show parties, suppers whatever. Looking back it was the relief of realizing that despite having been ill I could still work, could still

reach into the hearts of the people who paid to hear me speak. The people who felt that I could help them to understand that it is possible to lead more positive lives. In other words I had recovered from having two small strokes, my fear was evaporating. Staying in a hotel in a major English city I took a stroll around the shops. In a side street I found one of those old fashioned pen shops. A notice at one side of the window explained that this was also a pen hospital.

The pens I now own were simply there in the window. Green Waterman pens. As I looked at them I thought of Henry himself rushing down the road to buy ink in order for his client to sign the contract. Imagine his disappointment when he found he had missed his chance.
Did he sit and sulk, pull on his bottom lip or moan saying 'woe is me!' Not a bit of it. He gave himself a goal. He would change his life even if it necessitated him becoming an inventor. He solved the problem. A man with a goal. Necessity became the mother of invention. Of course I bought the pens. The fountain pen is used every day filled with its usual green ink. It gives me great pleasure.

So many of us need symbols in our lives. Objects, trinkets, treasures, even the torn off stub of a theatre ticket or a night at the opera. Someone I know quite well describes herself as a minimalist yet she has kept the programme for every theatre show that she and her husband have seen. 'But I keep nothing' she says. 'I am not a hoarder'.

Although when pressed she admits that tiny garments worn by her newly born children can still be found in her home. Out of sight yet not out of mind!

These invaluable things trigger our memories. They can be used to reassure us to keep us in touch with our innermost self. Although residing in the past can, if we spend too long there, inhibit our progress to the future it often helps us to achieve our goals.

Make yourself comfortable. Sit in your favourite chair. A glass of wine or a cup of tea in hand, give yourself permission to stop. Turn off your mobile phone, put your 'singing and dancing' latest computerised gadget in another room. This is your time. A time to be still, despite whatever else is happening in your life at that moment. Sit quietly and simply be yourself, it will not take up much time in your busy day.

Take out your box of memories and revisit for a while. Recharge your batteries. Touch again the trinkets that you have kept for years, the old photograph that you keep separate from all the others in your photo albums. A snapshot with a special story, an image of someone that you loved long ago. The paper heart that a boy at school gave to you on Valentine's Day, your father's old army medal, a button from the uniform you once wore yourself. A thin piece of ribbon. All our mementoes are different. Unique and special to us.

Your box of memories will be valuable, long after you are gone.

Can you hear their voices somewhere out there in the future, the voices of those you loved, who loved you in return and love you still.
'Did he keep that?'
'Here's my first drawing from nursery, grandad's medal and who is this in the photograph.'
'Just like my sister to hang on to .... almost everything.'
It was William Morris who said 'only have things around you that are beautiful or useful'.

Your box of memories has a beauty all its own!

The Escape

The door was slightly open. A shaft of sunlight brightened a cosy interior. The russet coloured carpet matched the fallen autumn leaves that covered the surrounding lawn and paths. The edge of a cushion was visible, old, well worn. The corner of a table, rough hewn on which sat a steaming mug of tea. This is Tom's garden shed. Tom's special place, his hideaway. The place where he sits, drinks tea and engages himself in the mysteries that only those who own a garden shed can truly understand On entering I become aware that the name 'shed' seems inappropriate for this very special place, surely it's much more than that.

There are two chairs both looking incredibly comfortable and as Tom rises from one to greet me I realise that here is a man who takes great pride in this cosy place. Within seconds the kettle is on. No mod cons for Tom, a tiny old fashioned primus stove is lit. He invites me to sit down. Tom explains that he does have a power supply in his hideaway but prefers to give 'body' to his memories, explaining that when he was a boy one of the joys of camping was using a primus stove. As we talk I notice shelves filled with old tobacco boxes all matching with neat little labels. Tools hang on homemade racks. Plant pots stand in the corner, tidy, nothing here unkempt or out of place. He follows my gaze and smiles. 'Like to keep it all in order' he says 'like when I was in the army'. The back of the shed has been extended making it much bigger. To one side there is a workbench, to the other a specially made table on which to 'pot his plants'. Tom has made shelves and surfaces in the most unlikely places, a tiny triangular shelf bridges a corner, it is just big enough to house a small radio. High above the window there is a shelf with ends that can be adjusted, 'for my books' says Tom. 'Just one or two but I like to have them close by.' Producing a second mug Tom makes my tea, time flies as we talk of many things, the past, the present, children, hobbies, gardens and of course sheds!

Later that same afternoon I shared yet another cup of tea with Dulcie, Tom's wife. We sat in the lounge with its chintz and antiques. 'For years' she said 'I used to wonder what on earth he did in there. Yes the garden is lovely but whenever I go down he is just sitting, thinking, sometimes scribbling with those funny stubs of pencils he has, or reading, always with a cup of tea at his elbow. He is in there for hours, even in the winter he has a heater. Can you imagine he leaves the comfort of our lounge to sit in his shed. Still, keeps him out of mischief I suppose, especially since he retired'.

The garden shed. Oh the magic of it all!

When I was a child we had a garden shed, my father escaped in much the same way as Tom, in fact when the pitch of my mother's voice rose higher and higher my father would edge towards the back door. As she turned away or stopped to take a breath he would be gone. It was as quick as that. Often she would shout 'Joe, Joe' but her words fell on deaf ears, he had already gone. Then she would turn to me. 'Don't think you're going to get away as easily'. But he, sweet man, had already escaped to his shed!

Dad's shed was not as comfortable as Tom's, albeit there was a small piece of carpet and a strange rickety chair that had once had its home indoors. When I was in there with my father I sat on a box. Sometimes my friend Edward from up the road came in and we would watch my dad working at his bench. He made stools, boxes, shelves, all sorts of things. When Edward and I were together we both sat on boxes, Dad said it kept us out of the way. He had of course made the boxes dual purpose, 'everything has to have more than one use' he would say. Edward believed that when he grew up he would have a garden shed, he bemoaned the fact that his dad didn't have one. My dad said that this might be due to the fact that he worked down the mine and preferred his greenhouse instead of a shed. The latter being more light and bright. It made sense, after all Edward's dad did spend most of his life in the dark underground.

Many of us need a place to escape. A place in which we can feel safe. As children we make make-shift houses out of blankets and old curtains and of course we must not forget the 'Wendy house'. The enjoyment experienced by small children playing

house has never changed, it has been part of life for decades. Little girls pretending to make tea and now in this enlightened age assisted by little boys. 'Dens' are made outdoors fashioned from tree trunks, old wood, fallen branches, they are not exactly garden sheds but surely the idea is much the same.
I asked Tom if he had ever made 'dens' as a boy. He smiled a long lingering smile. 'Dens' he said 'of course, we all made dens....' At that a wistful look came into his eyes.......as I left him in the solitude of his shed.

Could it be that the garden shed, your garden shed, provides you with your very own special escape from the stresses and strains of everyday living?

By the way, the sale of garden sheds has increased particularly during the last five years........... I wonder why?

Our greatest glory is not never falling, but in rising every time we fall

Confucius

King's Cross

We move in silence yet smile hesitantly as we brush against each other in the cramped space. Beyond the wall, London's traffic rolls past just as before yet with a distinct and noticeable lack of tooting horns. Declaring as it does that life goes on despite everything that has happened.

The sun shines, it is hot, sweaty, no breeze to lighten the heat yet still the pilgrims come one after the other carrying their flowers to place at the King's Cross shrine. Unexpectedly I, the true professional, whose control switch of emotion is so well ordered, find myself crying. Those silent tears that we weep when faced with immeasurable and unspeakable tragedy.

The flowers lie layer upon layer wilting in the sun crying out for water. Bouquets, posies, simple wild flowers, all can be found here each with a message. The written words speak volumes. There is no discrimination, no accusation, no bitterness, only tangible proof of empathy displayed in rainbow colours echoing the emotions and feelings. All is expressed here in an effort to give comfort and support to those who grieve.

A makeshift altar, candles, handwritten messages, pictures, flags pinned to the walls next to children's simple drawings and their hesitant little messages. I find myself enfolded within the warmth and the love. There is a sense of unity, of stubborn determination to be strong, of belonging. The will to survive is almost tangible. All around me, through these simple signs of grieving, comes a message loud and clear telling me that we will survive. We must survive.

A girl stands overcome by the scene in which she finds herself. In her hands three giant sunflowers, their heads held proud. Nearby a man prays audibly, he speaks a language I do not understand but here we are all as one, a woman cries, a young girl simply stands totally immobile as if like Lot's wife she is cast in salt. People shuffle past her in the limited pathway between the flowers, a space becoming narrower by the minute as more and more tributes arrive. There is a timelessness about this place as though on entering we become, inwardly, still. Strangely strengthened, finding an uneasy peace beside each other.

We come to mourn our dead, yes **our** dead, yours and mine though they may not be part of our immediate family. They are still ours, they belong with us, part of the family of this country and mankind. Bending I put my plant amongst the layers of flowers, it slips, I pick it up, it falls again, I look around trying to find a place where it can safely perch and in so doing find my tears falling on its leaves and on the tiny card which bears the message 'We must never lose heart, we must always unite'.

My tears are for all those who grieve, for those who wait, for those who still toil in the tunnels beneath the ground continuing to gather evidence. For the mothers of children who will never come home, for the wives of men who loved them, for the brothers, the sisters, the cousins, the friends, the fathers and

I weep for all of them, for everyone affected by this tragedy.
Who would not be touched by this senseless outrage?
Beyond the gates the police officers are courteous, understanding. They speak in soft voices, firm but fair. I wish them well as patiently they help as many people as they can. The traffic continues to gives its message of survival, London life goes on but sadly not for those who died here, nor will life ever be as it was for those who mourn, or to a lesser degree for any of us..
You will not be forgotten, you must always be remembered for you, all of you, are part of the family of life.

Joe

Recently I counselled Joe, a man in his early forties, who had pursued his career for over 20 years.

He said that he and his wife had a problem, "a domestic" he said, "we've got our very own domestic."

He then went on to describe the way in which he had snapped, losing his temper completely, charging off into his cellar after a small argument. There flailing around with a large piece of wood, breaking some of his tools and belongings.

"She's so different" he said, "she's nothing like the girl I married."

The argument had been caused over a very small incident. He had put something down, but when returning to the place where he was sure he had left it, it was gone. He accused his wife of moving it.

"You see, it's not just about that" he continued, "she's not the girl I married. She never laughs. When first we met she had such a wonderful sense of humour, she laughed and joked. It was great to be with her, now she's so different, she never has any energy for anything" he said, rather meaningfully.

I asked him how many hours a day his wife worked.

"Oh" he said, "she's got this really boring job, works on

a VDU, but that's not the problem, she's just changed, she's always nagging. The day it happened I had really had enough, I am sick and tired of her moving my things then pretending that she has never touched them, now, well, I can't be doing with her any more."

"Does she make your meals" I asked.

"Of course" he said.

"Does she wash and iron?"

"Obviously" he scoffed.

"Does she make arrangements for the children?"

"Oh yes" he said dismissively, "she does all of those things, but she's not the girl I married."

This man had never had an affair. He had never felt that he wanted to. During our counselling session never once did he suggest that he had considered leaving his wife.

"But" he repeated constantly, " She is not the girl I married".

I looked at this middle-aged man, his hair greying at the temples, his face showing signs of ageing. Did he still see himself as the callow youth he was then they first met? Did he ever look in the mirror and see what I could see?

After a pause I asked him if he was the person that she had married. He looked incredulous at my remark.

"Well, of course not" he said, "we all get older, how could I be the same person" then he laughed, "when we first met I was sixteen, she's a bit older than me, you know, she was eighteen. It seemed such a big age difference then but of course it's not much now, I hardly ever think about it." Another little laugh. "I couldn't possibly be like that. When I look back I was so stupid, my friends thought it foolish of me to want to settle down so soon, we were married by the time I was nineteen. We've had our whole lives together."

"So" I said, "If we look at the picture of your life, you are an older man, you complain that she is not the girl you married, did you wish as a middle-aged man to be married

to a young girl?" He looked very thoughtful.
"Of course not" he said.
We then reviewed his conversation.
"I'm different to what I was then" he said reflectively.
"Is she not allowed to be different also" I asked.
He hung his head. "I never thought about it like that, but, she could go to the hairdressers a bit more, she could be smarter if she tried, now she never seems to bother."
"What is her favourite colour?"
"Colour?" he said, "colour, well, I don't know, I would have to think about that, I'll ask her when I get back."
"No" I said, "do you remember her favourite colour?"
He thought for a long time. "I've no idea" he said, "I don't suppose I have ever known, though once, when she was twenty one I remember that at her twenty first party she wore a bright yellow dress. She rather liked herself in that, come to think of it. I don't think I remember her wearing that colour since, but she must have liked it at the same time because she went on about it, I remember quite distinctly."
"When did the two of you last take a walk together?"
"A walk? We've got the car"
"No, a walk together, when did you last walk on a beach holding hands? When did you last plan a day out, just the two of you?"
"Well" he said "there are always the children, we had them late you know, wanted to get on our feet first, they are always around."
"Are there relatives?"
"Oh yes, my mum's getting on but she loves to have them."
"When did you last take a stroll together, holding hands?"
He hung his head. "Well, I've been tied up with work" he said, "doing a lot of overtime, getting money together. We bought this house you see, bit of a dream really, needed a lot doing to it, not structurally mind you, but a lot of re-

wiring and re-plumbing. It's got difficult lately, not enough money. Everytime I look at the house it seems to want something else, I promised her a new kitchen, that was three years ago. We've never ever got round to it and now the eldest boy is taking his 'O' levels and we've got to think about university and all of that. I don't suppose she'll ever get her new kitchen, not unless I win the Pools."

"What does her life look like to you now?" I said, "married to a middle-aged man with whom she spends little time alone, who doesn't even know her favourite colour."

"You know," he said "sitting here in this quiet green room it all looks different, I came in almost hating her and now I want to go home and ask her what her favourite colour is."

This couple had made choices all along the way. I am not for one moment suggesting that the wife was easy to live with. Probably their lack of communication had led them to a precipice, over which both of them were hanging, tenuously, by their finger nails, neither able to help the other, only just managing to hold on.

He brought his wife to the second session. Her face was lined, she looked ten years older than her chronological age. She was in tears almost immediately.

"I promised myself I wouldn't do this" she said "I've no time for people who can't sort themselves out."

Half-an-hour later the three of us were attempting to do the sorting together. She had lost touch with him in just the same way that he had ceased to communicate with her. They spoke 'at' and talked 'to' but never chatted 'with' each other. They had lost sight of the deep needs of their own relationship.

Together we looked at the future, at what they wanted. They were able to appreciate that there are no rehersals for life. We just get the one chance!

Miraculously, through it all, they still loved each other. Both talked longingly of the past and as they did so their eyes shone, they looked sheepishly at one another.

"The harvest is still there" I said "it needs to be reaped." Although the seeds were planted an age ago, somehow through all the storms the crop had grown. They went away to reap.

As I opened the front door for them they hardly said goodbye to me. They walked up the street, she at first shyly linking him then he, big strong man, removed her arm gently and put his arm about her shoulders. She being much smaller, looked up into his face, he gently, shyly, fleetingly, kissed the top of her head, and they were gone around the corner, out of my life.

We are all given choices. Choices to decide what we want to do. Whether to hold grudges, storing them up, weaving them into a garment that we can wear constantly, never taking it from our back, or making the choice to live for the day, to plan a little for the future and to cherish that which is ours.

Very Special People

During my years working in Europe's second largest psychiatric hospital I met many people whose emotional bank balances were overdrawn. In some cases these lovely people had not had a credit or a deposit in their banking system for years and years. Eventually they had become institutionalised, never to be in fully in credit again. Faced with the experience of daily withdrawals such was their hardship, they devised ways to survive.

Very small aspects of their lives took on a major importance, their little rituals became precious to them; an act of kindness by a particular member of staff would be treasured and remembered.

Truly remarkable their stories are humbling yet reassuring. The next two chapters are about two of them, Billy and William.

'Patience is a virtue......'

Billy

Billy spent his days with his head bowed, gaze averted, sweeping the corridors of the psychiatric hospital which had been his home for many years. Billy was a mute; at least, that's what everyone believed; that's what he wanted them to believe. But patients are not always what they seem.

This is the story of Billy. I met him some years ago in a large psychiatric hospital. I had applied for a senior post and after being short-listed was called for interview in the company of seven other people. One of the senior nursing staff was given a task of taking us on a tour of the hospital. We walked from ward to ward, department to department; the day seemed endless. Our guide talked incessantly, most of the time about the history of psychiatry and the well-being of patients, and the way which the care of such patients had changed over the years, so that psychiatry could no longer be classed as the Cinderella of the service.

After some hours, we came to a large, long, drab, empty corridor; there were doors all the way along one side, and standing in the middle of the emptiness was an elderly man with sweeping brush in hand. His head was tucked well down and he appeared to be looking intently at particles of dust beneath the bristles of his brush.

As we approached he seemed not to notice us at all and went on diligently sweeping and sweeping, always in the same place. I looked at him for some considerable time, but he made no attempt whatsoever to raise his head or to answer my gaze. On seeing me doing this, our guide said quite cheerily: "This is Billy; Billy's very happy here with us, aren't you Billy?"

He patted Billy on the head as though he was a small child. No further words were said as we walked down the corridor. By then the guide was talking incessantly once more.

I looked back, and, over my shoulder saw Billy watching us. The senior nurse looked at me and said:

"Don't worry about Billy, Billy is mute, he hasn't spoken for over 20 years; he is one of those people who is very contented with his lot."

As the tour continued, I wondered if our guide knew Billy intimately. Did he spend hours talking to him? Did he really know?

Some weeks later, having received a letter telling me that the post was mine, I started work. It seemed that every day I would pass down that same drab corridor, and Billy would be there sweeping. Every time I passed Billy, I spoke to him.

"Good morning, Billy; Good afternoon, Billy; how are you, Billy?" There was never a response.

Days turned into weeks, weeks into months, I enjoyed my work. It seemed amazing to me that I could be paid for a job in which almost every minute was enjoyable.

I have always believed that it is impossible to measure with any certainty the true response of another human being, and because of this Billy became a challenge. I would sit on the window-sill close to him, chattering away as though we were having a two-way conversation. Billy swept on as though I wasn't there at all.

But one day a remarkable thing happened. It was to change my relationship with Billy. As I was leaving the house, the postman handed me some letters. I hastily popped them into my bag and took them to work with me, and on arrival opened them together with the department mail. Unfortunately, one of the letters contained some bad news. I was to report immediately to another hospital to undergo a rather serious operation. I had known for some time that this operation might be necessary, but suddenly to realise that I was summoned, as it were, immediately, was quite daunting.

I called in my staff and explained that I would be away for at least three months, and that we must spend the day trying to get things in order. This we did for a couple of hours, and then feeling rather glum, I decided to visit one of the geriatric wards, as this always seemed to cheer me up. I passed down the corridor as usual, visited the old ladies, and then on my way back to the office, I passed Billy. As I passed close to him, his hand came out and touched mine. For the very first time, I found myself looking into his blue, blue eyes. As soon as I looked at him, he looked away, withdrew his arm from mine, and mumbled:

"You didn't speak! you didn't speak to me today."

I was so surprised, that I wondered as I looked at

Billy's head once more bowed down, as he intently brushed the dust at his feet, if, in fact, I had dreamt that he had spoken and touched me. One or two people passed up the corridor, and Billy said no more, but when we were once more alone, I touched his arm and said:

"Billy, you can speak, you can really speak Billy."

He nodded his head and drew me to the side of the corridor, and carefully opening one of the doors, beckoned to me to follow him inside. I did so.

"Something is wrong," he said, without looking at me at all. "Something is wrong with you today."

"Yes." I said. "I'm going into hospital."

"I knew there was something wrong, I always know."

"Billy." I said, "Why is it that everyone thinks that you are mute?"

"That's a long story," said Billy.

"I'm going into hospital, I'm afraid."

"Don't be afraid," said Billy.

"Will you still talk to me when I get back," I said. He shrugged his shoulders, and then I asked:

"Why did you choose to talk to me? Why did you choose today?"

"Today was different," said the old man. "Today you were sad. I can always tell when people are sad by the number of steps they take up the corridor. People walk differently when they are sad. You walked differently today."

"Thank you for speaking to me," I said, "thank you so much."

Billy gave a wry smile.

"That's all right," he replied, "you always speak to me. Everyday — morning Billy; afternoon Billy; night Billy, you always speak."

"Am I worth trusting, Billy?" He shrugged his shoulders again.

"When I come back Billy, please talk to me again."

He pushed me gently through the door but remained in the room, as though he was afraid for both of us to be seen coming out together. I returned to my office, completed my work, went home and prepared for my stay in hospital.

During the weeks that followed, I gave much thought to my conversation with Billy. During the painful times it paled into insignificance, I began to believe it had never happened, and that I had been given to flights of fancy and imaginings. But three months later I was back at work, as chirpy as ever, and on the first day I walked down the corridor and there, as if there had been no span of time in between, stood Billy, brush in hand, sweeping just the same as ever.

I waited until the corridor was quite empty, and then I walked up to him.

"Hello Billy," I said, "I'm back, I'm better, would you like to go for a walk." There was no reply, no look, no glance, no shrugging of the shoulders, no lifting of the head, nothing.

Everything was just as it had been, the first time we had ever met.

"Oh Billy," I said, "Oh Billy," and then Billy said quietly:

"I'd like to go out, just for a walk."

A few days later, with the charge nurse's permission, Billy and I went walking in the grounds. The charge nurse was very glad, he said that someone was taking an interest in Billy, for Billy had no one who cared for him at all, apart from the staff, who liked him because he was quiet. It was they who brought him presents at Christmas, and on his birthday, it was they, the nurses, who made arrangements for his birthday cake, it was they who tried to make the ward like home.

We walked around the grounds, and then as we came to a deserted track, Billy asked:

"You've got a car?

"Yes" I replied.

"I'd like to go out please."

So the following week, Billy and I went out for a drive, and it was on the banks of a nearby river that Billy told me his story and explained to me why he had decided to be mute.

It is not a pleasant story, it belongs far back in time.

It belongs in the thirties, in what was the old asylum.

It belongs in a ward with 130 beds, and a foot of space between each one, because it was to this environment that Billy was admitted.

He had little knowledge or memory of his life before that, other than that he had been a teacher and lived at home with his mother and father, and then he commented:

"I think I had what they call a breakdown, and one day I was here. There was a lot of noise in the ward - a great deal of noise; shouting, shuffling, banging, screaming. It seemed to me that it was all noise, all terrible, terrible noise."

In those days, apparently, there were no trained nurses, only attendants who, for very small wages, looked after the inmates.

Billy had been in the ward for a very short time, when a large, burly male attendant approached him.

"Hello Jones," said the attendant. "What football team do you support?" Billy remembered that he smiled and said "Blackburn Rovers."

"Oh dear," frowned the attendant, and Billy found himself dragged away and placed in a most terrible, terrible room.

"I knew afterwards what it was called," he said, "The Pads."

Even now, in the warm sunlight, sitting on the banks of the river, a picnic lunch between us, even here with all the security and warmth, Billy obviously felt fear, saying "The Pads". "I hated it," he said, "I was sure I would die."

Eventually the door was opened and Billy was taken out. He was given a drink and then after about an hour, the attendant approached him again.

"Which football team do you support," he said.

"Blackburn Rovers," said Billy, and then it was once more, the terrible, terrible room. Sitting on the river bank, Billy's words did not come easily, they came with effort, with stuttering, great pauses.

Billy wasn't sure how long he spent in the padded cell at that time, but when he came out, another man appeared to be in charge, and he led Billy away, away from the padded cell.

Billy looked around the ward; he felt hurt and confused. Trying to escape from the noise, he looked for a quiet corner and then he saw a man sitting on a bed at the far end of the ward. On his bed were five withered brown leaves, for it was autumn, and the man was touching the leaves, with great reverence. Billy went over to him.

"What football team do you support," he said to the man.

The man smiled, without looking at Billy — an empty smile. "Queens Park Rangers," he replied.

"Thank you," said Billy. After that, life became easier for Billy. The next day when he was asked about his football preferences, he named the right team.

"Good on you," smiled the burly attendant. "You've learnt the rules already," and he patted Billy heartedly on the back.

"It was really then," explained Billy, "that I decided, it was a very strange world that I'd entered and that if I were mad, this place was about a kind of madness, much more mad than I."

He endured the life that the asylum had to offer for some years, and then one day, could endure it no longer.

"It was then I decided not to speak," he said. There were tears running down his face, I took out a tissue, and wiped them away.

"Have you had enough talking for one day, Billy?" I asked. He nodded. "Do you ever talk to anyone?"

"Yes" he replied. "I talk to the cats, they're all over the grounds you know, dozens of them. I talk to the birds and I talk to one or two of the patients, the ones that everyone thinks are very, very mad. It's all right to talk to them, you see, because if they said that I could speak, no one would believe them; we are all just patients."

Billy and I spent many many hours together. Billy knew everything there was to know about hospital life; he knew where everything was kept, he knew which members of the staff loved other members of the staff, which husband was meeting whose wife, he knew when the consultant was late on his rounds, and he knew the staff who arrived late in the morning. He noticed if they had hangovers, but he noticed most the staff who really cared.

He told me of one nurse, who always gave him extra sugar in his tea, because she said: "As you don't talk, Billy, I don't know how much sugar you take. But the sugar will do you good and give you energy." Billy liked her. He liked, too, those members of staff who, as he said, "kept themselves smart. That's how nurses should look."

I asked Billy if I could write about him, if I could tell his story. At first he said:

"No — no I wouldn't like that." But then he decided "In 10 years I will be very old or dead, and if you want to tell my story then, you can. No one will listen, Vera; no one really cares."

There isn't a lot I can say, now, about Billy. His story is told. What strides have been made in psychiatry? There are now psychotropic drugs and deep in-group therapy, to say nothing of psycho-analysis, home-leave and rehabilitation. Group homes in the community flourish and elderly disturbed people strive to make new lives in the community. But for the Billys of this world, all this progress, this futuristic look at what mental illness is about, is too late. For they remember the years of suffering, of misunderstanding, of ignorance, but in Billy's case, they were also years of ingenuity, of using a mind that had always been bright, to its best purpose.

Billy, who at a very early age could read and write, had in fact been to university and obtained a degree; he was a clever man, who found himself in an unfriendly climate. But he, with his brightness of spirit, took out his survival kit and used it. We praise great explorers, who conquer nature, who achieve great things. But to my mind, Billy is one of the greatest of them all, he explored a facet of human nature and behaviour, that perhaps no one hitherto had seen. He became mute by choice. He chose to whom he would speak. Not for him the social hypocrisy of life. For him only the pain of truth.

During our last conversation Billy said:

"It's safe to talk to some people, because they have love in their faces and dangerous to talk to others, because there is only hardness there."

Billy taught me so much. He made me feel humble. He had so many answers, so much perception, so much insight into the human condition. But most of all he had so much courage. He made his choices and lived by them - he managed to survive.

During the time I spent working in psychiatry I was privileged to meet Billy and others who had spent many years as patients in a large psychiatric hospital.

Into my life they not only brought wisdom but a deeper knowledge of meaning of the word survival. I am humbled by their dignity.

God moves in a mysterious way
His wonders to perform
He plants his footsteps in the sea,
And rides upon the storm.

William Cowper.

William

It was bitterly cold, the four of us were drenched to the skin but still William would not move.
"Can't" he said.
"Can't, must go, voices say must go back."
William, the most gifted of musicians, standing in the rain listening to the voices in his mind.
"Must go now!"
Sam, small, mesmerised and cold said "I'll go with him."
Jim stared blankly into the night and still it rained.
We were standing outside a Village Hall on a wet cold November night. The three men wore lounge suits under their sodden raincoats whilst I, clutching a small umbrella knew that the rain had already seeped through my coat onto my dress.
The rear door of the hall was open, a light shone upon us. A harassed female came out yet again for what seemed the hundredth time.
"Please" she said, "what's happening, the hall is packed, they have waited for twenty minutes already, we will have to say something."
She began to wring her hands "Oh dear." She said.
"We should never have got involved with you and these patients. We will have to return all the ticket money and it's just as I thought."
She, feeling the rain falling on her head stepped into the doorway.
"Well I am not getting soaked," she said. "If you want to stand there all night in the rain then that's up to you!"

William looked at me. The raindrops running down his lovely thin featured face.
"Sorry must go back, she says no!"
I knew that he was not referring to the woman in the doorway but to one of his voices.
In desperation I wondered yet again how to combat these tortuous voices, to rescue William who played his violin so well that listening audiences were stunned by his genius. At first they were silent and then broke into tumultuous applause.
"Which side?" I said. "Where is the voice coming from?"
He turned his head and looked over his left shoulder. In desperation I picked up a stick and said "William, I am stronger than her. All the people inside the hall are waiting to hear you play. We must go in. I am going to get rid of your voice. I am going to knock her down." I swept the stick over his shoulder as though I was knocking an offensive burden to the ground and then I jumped up and down on the invisible thing that had fallen down.
"Now" I said. "Take a deep breath, she's gone." He looked at me and smiled his lovely enigmatic smile. He stood for a while still smiling then suddenly said "Right" and in we went.
Behind the stage I combed his wet hair and Sam's and Jim's and eventually my own. My tights splattered with mud, my dress wet across the shoulders. We sallied forth onto the stage, a Quartet with a difference. Where did it all begin? For William it began because he was a musical genius who played the violin at three years of age.

From then on he began to live for his music. Deprived of an ordinary childhood through no fault of his own or indeed his parents he became so easily a victim of his own youthful success. Eventually he began to feel complete only when he was as one with his violin. He told me how he could not sleep without the violin and as often children hug soft teddies, he held tightly to his musical companion until he could think of little else. He sought not success, prowess or money but he said "the music gives me peace." William and I met long after his boyhood days. He was by then a man in his late fifties who spent endless days staring into space in a mental hospital. An asylum, a people's sanctuary for those who communicate with us in a different way. So different that many people in the outside world are afraid to respond. A place where he was no longer encouraged to be a musician, a place where people believed that his gift was responsible for his mental state. He spoke little, simply sitting, staring, and sometimes walking in the grounds of the hospital. His locker housed a scratched and battered violin with broken strings. Always when we met he smiled as though his life consisted of staring and smiling, walking and taking his tablets. Noise from troubled patients in his ward made him feel afraid, even twenty five years of asylum life had not equipped him to cope with any form of emotional pain.

Our conversations began. When trust had grown between us he told me of his beloved music. Eventually with encouragement he began to play again. After a while the now repaired, once broken, violin was replaced with a newer one and the hesitant strains of his fingering filled the ward. Others did not appreciate his need or his gift and consequently new private places had to be sought so that he could play. There were amongst the very clever experts those who believed that by playing again William would have a relapse. William proved them wrong.

His voices came and went as they always had.

Some days "she" told him he could not play and on other days "she" was silent and he played like an angel.

One day whilst he was playing a shuffling was heard outside the door, the feet stopped and then shuffled on and then came again and again. The man on the corridor heard the strains of music, opened the door and simply said "I can play too." And so he could.

Painstakingly and with great care his elderly fingers caressed the strings with love and hesitancy. His name was Jim. Pedantically he sought to make the music of his youth. He knew that unlike William he had never had the gift of genius, however, he could provide a stringed support for William and so the formation of our little music group began.

Searching to increase their number I found Sam. Piano playing, muttering Sam and as for me I simply sang a little Our concerts in the community began and two years pleasure was given to many elderly people. William, Sam, Jim and I enjoyed the giving. It proved to be a remarkable experience, however, eventually, because of age and weariness the period of our delight was curtailed. Then suddenly Sam died. We all felt bereaved not only had we lost Sam but we had lost his piano playing which had improved with every performance. Though William and Jim remained they did not recover from the loss of their companion but still sometimes there could be heard the strains of music on the corridors of the asylum.

The music fells on the ears of the receptive and uncaring – but still they played.

When Jim died William played no more. William had made his choices as did Sam and Jim. They let their music come to life and William had once more relived his genius. He took his gift and cradled it in his hands until it escaped to his fingertips and caressed the strings of his violin. William too has long since gone but I can still, in my mind, in my heart and in my head hear once again the sound of his music and visualise his lovely thin featured face, as always smiling his enigmatic smile.

Sometimes we complain for little or no reason, somehow missing the point of life. But we are alive. For these three men, life was hope as they played their music once more.

The Girl's Story

The room was warm. She looked around. A typical hospital bed, next to it a locker and a screen to one side and a chair beside the window. The walls painted pale green. Through the window she could see trees and a few houses and then in the distance the Lake District hills.
She was alone and afraid; in a strange place where her father said she would find her senses, have a good rest and then they could get on with their lives. The three of them, together again. It would be as before.

He and her mother had arranged for her to have a period of convalescence after her bad experience and he assured his daughter that it would work 'like magic' because God was good and his faith in God never wavered.
The matron entered the room.
'How are you settling in dear?' Although she looked stern and remote in her crisp starched uniform her brown eyes were warm; the girl liked her and felt safe.
'Get into your nightie, you need a good rest after your journey. We need to take your temperature and your blood pressure. Nurse will be along shortly to do that and she will bring you a nice cup of tea and a biscuit.'
With that she closed the curtains although it was the middle of the day. Snug in her nightdress the girl smiled as a friendly nurse did what had to be done.

'Her bark is worse than her bite' she said of the matron 'but she really cares. She was lovely with me when my brother died'.
The tea tasted good and the biscuit, though plain, was just what she needed. Soon she fell fast asleep.

She dreamt of her life at the little house. Of her love for her husband, and in the dream he turned into a monster and screaming so loudly in her sleep she awakened herself to find the kindly matron stroking her head saying 'There, there, try not to fret, you are safe here. No one can hurt you.'
'How long did I sleep?'
'Hours my dear, it's time for tea. Sandwiches and home made rice pudding. As you missed lunch just let us know if you want extra. We will look after you and tomorrow nurse will help you to take a bath.'
She ate little. The rice pudding was tasty and she felt like a small child being cherished and then aided by a capsule of she knew not what she fell into a deep sleep.

The first few days passed all too quickly. She seemed to sleep most of the time, awakening only to eat a little and to take yet another blue capsule. 'Sleep is a great healer' said the middle aged doctor.
He had examined her bruises and then asked her lots of questions, the need for which remained a puzzle in her mind. He could see what had happened. Surely months of being beaten had left her seven stone frame black, blue and yellow but

now that part of her life was over and she need never go back to it.

The next morning she awakened early and tried to get to the bathroom as quickly as she could. She wanted to be sick; all these tablets, doubtless. The sickness persisted. The doctor came again and it was then that she heard the matron whisper 'she is not strong enough to be told yet and I insist that we wait until she is on her feet.'

Told what, she thought, as she faded once more into oblivion.

Two more days passed. She felt nauseous quite often and eventually when she was sitting in the chair beside the window, decided to talk to the nurse.

'As these tablets are making me so sick surely I should not be taking them ?'

'Doctor's changed them already, miss, to some that are safe.'

'Safe, safe! Were the others dangerous?'

At that point the matron and the doctor came into the room.

'We need to have a talk' he said.

'I am feeling better. I'm sure I will be back teaching in a few weeks. This rest has done me so much good.'

'You may well get back to school but you will have to take good care of yourself. You are going to have a baby.'

At first it was as though she was listening to the radio and someone had turned the volume down. She could hear the words from a great distance away.

'She's going to faint.'
'Lay her on the bed matron, this girl has really had enough'.

They were so kind. Whenever she thought of that day it was the absolute kindness that she remembered.
Later, left alone, she thought about her parents' reaction. They would be horrified. They already had dreams of her becoming a headmistress. Soaring to the top of her career. All of this to be after the Pope had granted her an annulment of her marriage.
The annulment... Oh God there would be no forgiveness now with a baby on the way.
After lunch she sat in the chair by the window watching the birds in a nearby tree....a baby....my very own baby. A baby to love and who will love me. I'll make all the baby clothes. I'm a good knitter. I'll use white or yellow or even pale green wool.
Suddenly all the pain she had felt over the past year and a half was gone and she found herself feeling joyful that she would have a baby of her own to love.
Later she would face the prospect of her mother's reaction but she had another two weeks to get used to the idea and to make plans for her baby's future. Her own baby!

What joy she would have; singing lullabies, changing nappies, rocking the baby, the cuddles. She would make sure that no one would ever hurt the life that she carried inside her.

'You are mine dear heart, dear little one. You are my precious.' She patted her tummy and from that moment talked to the baby as though she knew for certain it could hear.

Matron Williams had very firm ideas about convalescence and its relevance to the patient's recovery and it was her custom to speak at some length about the benefits of ozone.
To this end she would summon the local taxi driver, bid him bring his car to transport a patient who she felt sure would enjoy sitting on the sea front. The benefits of such an experience being immeasurable. And so it was that a week prior to discharge each patient was afforded this great treat. Sometimes more than one trip would be arranged.
This arrangement had been in place for years having commenced within a short time of her arrival.
So it was that the day arrived when the young mother-to-be was told to put on her coat for an outing. However, instead of watching the arrival of the usual taxi she saw drawing up at the front door a huge coach.
The matron was furious with the driver and although he explained that the taxi was being repaired and the other car was 'on a long run' she would have none of it.

Eventually after much argument she agreed that he could take the girl down to the sea front as usual. The coach drove slowly down the hill to the shore, its one passenger feeling like the Queen of Sheba!!

It was a beautiful day. The spring sunshine trying valiantly to push the cold winter air away. The driver turned on the heater and by the time they had parked at the edge of the estuary all was warm and cosy.

'Do you want an ice-cream, lass, or a cup of tea?' He pointed to a café on the other side of the road. 'Or you could even have both!' As he said this a smile crossed his face.

'My, you're a bonny lass, what are you doing yonder with all the old cronies, have you been ill for a long time?'

He brought the ice cream cornet and then went back for the tea and some biscuits. It was as though she had known him forever. At first he told her about his son and daughter 'about your age I think' he grinned. 'You look so sad ...'

That was how it began years ago with a simple statement of fact. 'You look so sad.'

Later, looking back, she tried to analyze why it had all been so easy. She talked and talked to this kindly man who concentrated so hard on what she was saying that he pushed his cap to the top of his head and then at one point took it off altogether.

She told him of the boyfriend who she had really loved, their engagement, the breaking of that relationship because both sets of parents were ardent members of different religions. The grieving, the loss that was followed by an allowed freedom that she had never known. She told him how she had felt walking into the Ritz ballroom in

Manchester with a girl from church who wasn't really a friend. A girl whose father was known to her father so that made it alright.

The driver hardly spoke. They drank their tea companiably as though they had known each other forever.

She stopped. A tear ran down her cheek. She looked at the face of the listener; she saw the kindness and was not surprised when he said gently 'what happened then?'

'I met this lovely, handsome, catholic man, a bit older than me. Mum and dad were delighted and his parents felt that we would make the perfect match, and within a year we were married.'

'It didn't work, there wasn't enough love and I couldn't cope with his tempers and soon he was seeing some one else. Being married made no difference he said.

'One night, well, it all got out of hand. For eighteen months he said he had put up with me but now it was over. He was very strong and, well, luckily someone found me and I am here now getting better.'

'Where is he?'

'Did a runner; it's all over and the Pope was going to give me an annulment so I can still go to mass, only now I don't suppose he will because I'm going to have a baby.'

The man turned sideways in his seat, the better to look at her face, to convince himself that the joy in her voice was truly just that. He need not have worried. She was so quietly pleased that she was to be a mother. Her face glowed and he could feel a

lump in his throat. Still tears lingered in his eyes 'another cuppa before they shut up for the day?'
The few out of season holiday makers had long since returned to their B&Bs seeking warmth and afternoon tea. A man walked a black labrador along the road. As she waited for the driver to return she felt as though a great weight had been lifted from her. Opening the window she breathed in the cold sea air as it blasted its way up the estuary. High above, seagulls valiantly flew, buffeted by the gusts and squalls. I am as free as you she thought. I will fly free.
The driver's door opened and there he was, the listener. The wise man who had known when and when not to speak and consequently had said so little.
A man who spent his life at the beck and call of others. She looked at his face as though she had not seen it previously. He smiled 'ee lass you'll do alright. You're a strong girl in here' he pointed at his head 'and in ere', he placed his hand on his heart.
'Will your parents look after you?'
'I'm scared of telling them but I don't think they will throw me out 'cos after all I am a married woman. They would worry what people at church would think if they did!

Back at the nursing home an anxious matron telephoned the familiar number of the taxi firm only to be told that the driver was out 'on a job'. 'I know that, it's a job for me'.

'But he's not back and it's getting cold. If that girl takes a turn for the worse... well.'
As she replaced the receiver she heard a car approaching but it wasn't just a car. The large coach lumbered up and stopped at the door.
'Well, you've taken your time. What on earth have you been doing? 'She will be frozen stiff?'
'Matron, don't take on. I wrapped her in blankets, started the engine on and off and she got the benefit of your precious ozone!'

As he helped the girl down the steps onto the drive he whispered
'You'll go far lass, just trust in your maker and yourself. It will all work out with you and the baby.'

Later that night as she laid in the cosy bed the mother-to-be asked herself what it was the man had done. What magic was it that had lifted the weight she had carried for so long?
At first she tossed and turned trying to work the puzzle out until at last she fell into a deep sleep. In her dreams she was a seagull flying high into the sky. Free and full of hope.

The next day the matron asked her if she could knit. I not only teach little children, matron, I teach crafts as well.'
'Well, you will make good use of this then.'
It was three balls of pale yellow baby wool and a pair of needles. 'I particularly like this pattern. A little present for you.'

Then becoming a little red in the face she bustled away.

As she began to look at the pattern the girl suddenly realized just what the man had done. With his cap askew, with the cups of tea and so little talk, he had given her a most precious gift. The gift of his empathy.
He had looked at life through her eyes.
He had listened for her sake and not his own.
He had made her believe that she was the most important person in his life and in so doing had restored her self esteem.
His final words of encouragement again had helped her to be strong. Most of all he had put his own life 'on hold'.
There was a magic about it and a discipline; they had sat for two hours and it had all been for her. She felt very special.

A week later and she was in the back of the taxi leaving the nursing home for the last time. The previous day she had managed to walk down the steep hill to the shop, bought some flowers for matron and after a fortifying cup of tea in the café climbed back up the hill.
She had spent long hours planning for the future. What she would do with her life. What kind of mother she would be and here she was on the way home to her parents. At the bottom of the hill she asked the driver if he would park for a few moments where they had parked days before.

He nodded and showed no surprise when she got out of the car. With her face turned towards the sea, looking across at the Lake District hills with their feathering of snow white against the blue sky she said in a voice louder than a whisper:

'Dear God I make a vow to you today as I stand here.
I solemnly promise you that I will spend the rest of my life helping others by listening to what they want to say. The doctors have helped me, my family have tried to help but this man sitting in the car behind me gave me what I needed most. He gave me his time, he listened, he strengthened me.
Dear Lord, that is what is missing in life. People need somewhere to go to, some person. I will be that person. Please give me strength, understanding and wisdom but most of all grant me empathy.'
She got back in the car; the driver smiled.
'I made a vow. Thanks to you I know what I have to do.'
He smiled 'you'll do fine lass; just fine.'

A year later the young woman returned to the same spot to renew the vow. She pushed a laughing baby before her in a push chair. 'We are taking the ozone, son' she said as she crouched beside him.
She continued to return every couple of years sometimes more frequently if she was working in the area.

Many years passed. Now she is a grandmother. She has three adult children and nine grandchildren, she writes books, still sings, enjoys patchwork and walking in the country. She is delighted when those she loves tell her that she is more than a trifle eccentric!
She has yet another labrador (there has been a succession of them over the years.)
She twice yearly visits the U.S.A. to give presentations and enjoys every minute. She has lectured in Australia, Germany and many other places meeting hundreds of people and signing books. She wakes each morning determined to seize each day!
Very often members of her audience ask her how she came to be a counsellor, after all she has been in practice forty years.
'I was one of the first' she replies, but rarely lets her audience know where it all truly began.
But now the truth is out at last.
Now you know.
I was that young woman and, yes, I still go back and stand in the same place and renew my promise. You see it is my 'right of passage, and after all as I say to the children in my life a promise is a promise is a promise.........!

Afterword

Here we are at the end of the book.

As I write this last piece the rain beats against the windows, my dog signals to me that she wants to be out walking, and I am reminded how lucky I am to be able to make simple choices in my life.

We can all enjoy ordinary everyday experiences, reminding ourselves that we have our own gifts and talents to contribute to life itself.

In my introduction I offered you strong tea and biscuits in the form of true stories.
Thank you for joining me.

Now it is time for me to put the teapot into the cupboard and the cups back on the shelf but only briefly as my next book is already taking shape in my mind and so I invite you to join in

'Another Cup'
More true tales to encourage and inspire

which will be available early next year.

Au revoir. Keep safe and well until next we meet.
God Bless.

Vera Waters
June 2007

'Yesterday is past...already gone...
Tomorrow is yet to come...
Today, this very special time is where we are now...
That is why it is called the present...because it is a gift.'

Vera Waters

Vera Waters' first two books, **Half a Rainbow** and **The Other Half of the Rainbow**, are now out of print. Her third book is

RECIPE FOR A RAINBOW
Inspirational Stories of Everyday Life

'Reading this book provides a release for one's imagination and a return to abundant thinking. Her wit and insight into everyday human life experiences translates into personal acceptance and freedom. Vera's wisdom and no-nonsense style is refreshing and pleasing to the heart.'

Rick Scruggs, Lynchburg, Virginia, USA

Recipe for a Rainbow is available from bookshops at £7.00 or direct from:
Penn Cottage Books, PO Box 121, Chorley, Lancashire PR6 8GF
Telephone 08707 651227 www.verawaters.com
Email vera.waters@virgin.net

Also available from Penn Cottage Books are two CDs that each cost £9.00. Postage is free for orders for books or CDs sent to Penn Cottage Books.

Vera Waters' CDs are:

LITTLE BY LITTLE...
Going forward in your life after the loss of a loved one can be the greatest challenge of all. This wise and comforting CD offers practical advice and guidance. Through her empathy and understanding, Vera Waters will help you to cope with the present as you face the future.

WHERE DO YOU KEEP THE GUITAR?
Many wish to live richer, more positive and fulfilling lives, but where do we find the time and encouragement to make the changes required to reach this goal?
Vera's straightforward, practical CD encourages us to 'seize the day' and offers commonsense and guidance in a world which sometimes leaves us feeling helpless and out of control.

Vera Waters is an inspirational speaker who you can book for your future events. Please contact Penn Cottage Books at the addresses opposite.